THE PRODIGAL DELIVERER

A True Story of God's Power in The Life of One Man

PETE BROWDER

The Prodigal Deliverer
Pete Browder

Copyright © 2016 by Pete Browder
PO Box 98
Centreville, AL 35042
www.theprodigaldeliverer.com
freedindeed@me.com

If you are interested in inviting Pete Browder to speak at your church or organization or for other ministry opportunities, feel free to contact him using the above information.

To receive updates regarding new publications by Pete Browder, go to www.theprodigaldeliverer.com and sign up for the newsletter.

First Published in the United States of America

First Printing: April 2016

All rights reserved. This book or any portion thereof may not be reproduced or used in any manner without the express written permission of the author except for the use of brief quotations in a book review.

All Scripture quotations are from the King James Version of the Bible.

ISBN: 978-0-9975057-0-2
Cover Design by Victoria Cooper

Dedicated to my mother and the One we serve

Acknowledgements

I am very thankful for the courageous people who gave me permission to share their marvelous stories as part of my testimony. My wife Sandy, my cousin Suzanna, and my sister have set aside all fears in lieu of unashamedly promoting the truth of Christ through the sharing of their experiences.

Special recognition to Zora Knauf for her outstanding editorial work on this project. Her assistance has been indispensable in helping me bring this book to completion.

I am also thankful for the artistic talent and services of Victoria Cooper, who graciously worked with me to design the book cover.

Table of Contents

Introduction

This book is a true story. My inspiration comes from the hope that there are others who can relate to and be inspired by my testimony. Overcoming my tendencies as a private person, I have made every effort to tell my story with honesty and integrity. Much of what I have to say involves painful personal failures and situations that are difficult for me to think about, much less put into writing and share publicly. However, I have striven to portray my experiences with straightforward authenticity. Real life is not always pleasant—it is often marked with pain and suffering. From that standpoint, what I have to share is very believable. However, many may find what I say hard to believe because of the numerous supernatural events that are an unmistakable part of my story.

I can say with all confidence that the same God who has revealed Himself to me desires to reveal Himself to you with powerful demonstrations of His presence. You can embark on a similar journey where you will come to genuinely know Him, be set free, receive a call to service, and be used to accomplish work for the Lord of eternal value. Do not delay reading this book. Get on the path to true happiness and fulfillment now by discovering what it means to have a *really* right relationship with your maker and His eternal benefits.

I was a prodigal who ventured from the protections of his Father and returned home just in the nick of time. My heavenly father delivered me from the hands of my enemies, set me free, and called me into ministry to do the same. Delivered by God and called to deliver. I am a prodigal deliverer.

Early Challenges

In 1971, my mother came home to find my father in their bed with another woman. She promptly packed essentials, fled the Atlanta area, and headed home to her parents' house in Tuscaloosa, Alabama along with me and my younger sister. As a three year old, this would be the last time that I would ever see my father alive.

As strange as it might seem, this awful situation was an answer to my mother's prayers. She had been hoping for a resolution to the chaotic situation in which she had been living. It had not always been that way. Her relationship with my father had begun with all the blessings of southern deity. My parents made a handsome couple with all the trappings of success. Both were from hardworking, high moral, educated, and God-fearing families. My mother was a member of Pi Beta Phi sorority and my father was the charismatic president of his fraternity, Sigma Alpha Epsilon, at the University of Alabama. In 1964, with all the proper credentials in place, my parents, Francis Peterson "Peter" Givhan, Jr. and Mallie Faye Lake, were married as juniors attending the University of Alabama.

From the time that my parents were married up until when they were separated in 1971, my mother had been snatched all over the southeastern U.S. It seemed that my father was on a quest to finish his education or find the right job. She had put her trust in a leader who could not make a decision and stay the course. She had come to believe that his reasoning and abrupt changes of direction were based on less than sound judgement. She needed a head of household that she could rely on for considerate leadership and financial support. Quite to the contrary, to follow his lead meant nothing more than scatterbrained chaos and instability. Many years later I would learn that there were other forces that were spurring him along. After graduation, he immediately enrolled in graduate school. After getting his masters in History, he then enrolled in an Austin, TX seminary for one semester. When that did not work out, he took a job as a history professor in Thomasville, GA. That lasted one semester and then they were back to UA with his intent to get a masters in Psychology. I had just been born, and the three of us were living in college housing when my mother got pregnant with my sister. With that news, the writing was on the wall and my father finally took a job as an insurance adjuster in Atlanta. Years later, the affair was the excuse she needed to leave him and make her escape.

My mother went back to college to somehow turn her home economics degree into something that would allow her to provide for me and my sister. Even though she never got any child support, she received faithful help from her family until she got on her feet. After a few years, she got her degree in special education and took a job teaching in Pensacola, Florida.

Just when mother's life was reaching a degree of normalcy, she heard me fall out of bed and to her dismay, I was laying in the floor shaking uncontrollably with a seizure. I was five years old and had never had any problems before so she was unsure if the fall had caused the seizure or if the seizure caused the fall. After deliberation, she took me to see neurologist Dr. Gabriel Fernandez in Druid City Hospital in Tuscaloosa for testing. Dr. Fernandez ordered that I receive an electroencephalogram (EEG). An EEG is a test that detects electrical activity in the brain by gluing wired metal discs in various locations on the scalp. I remember the process vividly as I was forced to sleep overnight all wired up in the hospital.

The results were not good. Dr. Fernandez concluded that the test pin-pointed epileptic activity caused by a bone spur in my brain. Worse yet, there was nothing that could be done to resolve the problem. He said that some young people who suffered from epilepsy could eventually grow out of it, but that my situation was irreversible and permanent. Dr. Fernandez counseled her that I would not be able to lead a normal life because I was vulnerable to having a seizure at any time. I would not be able to swim, drive, or do anything where a debilitating seizure might cause me to harm myself or others. I was prescribed a daily dose of phenobarbital, a seizure controlling barbiturate with a side effect of hyperactivity in children. I would take one little pill every night before bed. I was oblivious and very hyper but my mother was crushed.

Just when my mother was feeling overwhelmed from the weight of this situation, she got a call from Woody Browder. Woody lived in Eutaw, AL, a little town just outside of Tuscaloosa, where he worked for his father in a hardwood veneer business. Also a divorcee, Woody wanted to drive down to Pensacola and have a weekend date with my mother. Former swimmer and baseball player at University of Alabama, he was quite the specimen with broad shoulders and an outgoing personality. Woody was a very charismatic partier who made his rounds all over west Alabama. The local beer distributor would give Woody free cases of whatever brand he wanted to promote and let him do his thing. Rare were the times that a beer and ice-laden cooler was not in the trunk of his car.

My mother must have been quite lonely and agreed to the visit. The consummate ladies' man, Woody drove the 4 hours to see my mom, but much to his dismay found himself bunking with me. His party weekend on the coast turned into something much less than he planned. He would soon learn that my petite mother would be no easy conquest. Woody was used to getting what he wanted, but my mother told him matter-of-factly that he would have to get his life together if he wanted a shot with her. My mother's no-nonsense challenge woke him up.

After returning home, Woody soberly considered the mess he had made of his life and became deeply depressed. It was at this time that he planned to kill himself. Taking his life would not be difficult, except that he wanted his son and daughter to receive proceeds from a life insurance policy he had purchased on himself for them. The fine print of the insurance contract meant that if it was determined that he committed suicide, they would not pay. Woody devised a plan and determined to follow it.

As is common during the rainy winter months, the Black Warrior River was flowing fast and high, about 10 miles from the Eutaw city limits. Late at night, Woody drove out to one of the rural boat landings along the river which were always lonely places during the high river season. This time of year even the teenage window steamer uppers were unlikely visitors. As expected, he was all alone. Parked with a loaded pistol on the seat next to him and a case of liquid courage working its way through his system, he would soon be primed to finish the job. His plan was to soothe his nerves with alcohol, position himself precariously on the river's edge, and shoot himself in the head so that he would fall dead into the swift current. He figured that he would be 30 miles downriver before being missed and even further before his vehicle was found. With any luck, his death would be shrouded in mystery and result in some cash for his kids.

All was going according to plan and his decision was final. He was about halfway through his beer when someone appeared at the driver side window and said, "God said do not do it." Certain that he was the only human there and that he had not told anyone else of his plans, he was instantly convinced that whoever had spoken was not of this world. Whoever spoke to him literally scared the Hell out of him. He hurriedly cranked up, slammed the transmission into gear, and squealed tires as he left the boat landing.

Shortly after this incident, Woody received a surprise visit from the new Eutaw Methodist Pastor, Caddell, whose former church was in Camden where Woody grew up. Some of Woody's childhood buddies asked the pastor to look him up and invite him to their weeklong tent revival meeting on the outskirts of Eutaw. Woody decided to go and on the third night of the revival, after listening to his friends' testimonies, gave his life to the Lord.

Woody's life was forever changed by his new relationship with and commitment to God. He lost his taste for alcohol and turned his life around. He claimed that when my mother found out, it was she who propositioned him for marriage. They were married on August 20, 1975 and we moved from Pensacola, Florida to Eutaw, Alabama.

Life in the Browder household would be very different for me. I was a stubborn child who was used to being the little man of the house. Without a father figure around most of my life, I was in for a shock as Woody quickly taught me what discipline felt like. His belt was so long that he would have to fold it four times or else risk knocking stuff off the dresser while aiming for my rear-end.

My mother and stepfather immediately looked to go further in their relationship with God. They tried out several mainstream denominational churches in the area. No matter how small the town, churches are on every corner in the Bible Belt. As was common in those days, on Friday or Saturday nights we would go to all night singings in little country churches scattered throughout backwoods of Greene County. Initially they settled into Cumberland Presbyterian where they were married. My mother was raised a conservative First Presbyterian in downtown Tuscaloosa so this was a countrified version of what she was used to. My mother's father and mother, Gay and Irene Lake, rarely missed church, and she had a solid Christian upbringing.

When Woody was a party man, he was no holds barred. Now as a Jesus man, he had the same enthusiasm but with a very different cause. He had tried all the world had to offer and would have been dead if not for God's intervention. Now he wanted all that God had to offer. Cable TV had come to town and my parents began watching religious programming like Pat Robertson and Kenneth Copeland. In 1980, Woody saw advertising for the Washington for Jesus demonstrations, rallied by Pat Robertson and other religious leaders. On a whim, he decided to buy tickets to Washington on the Amtrak train that stopped right there in Eutaw to board my mother and him. My mother was made immediately uncomfortable by the unusual number of Christian fanatics who had already boarded the train before reaching Eutaw. Conservative and introverted by nature, my mother braced herself as she got on the train for a long weekend with these strange types who were beside themselves about making a stand in Washington for Jesus. They were praying, singing hymns, and basically having church all the way to Washington. Mother was not having any part in the festivities until she found herself listening in on a conversation between a few men who were discussing somebody who had been miraculously healed. Immediately her thoughts went to me and my debilitating epilepsy. Instantly she overcame her shyness and interrupted them. She wanted to know if God had really healed someone. The answer she got from these gentlemen was a resounding *yes* as they offered her further testimony. She shared her need and they offered to pray with her. She accepted and they stepped outside onto the back porch between rail cars for some privacy. One man was praying in an unknown tongue while the other in English. Unable to close her eyes, she just stared at them. She did not know if God was still doing miracles, but she was all out of options. Before the end of the trip, my mother would make a deal with God. She told Him, "If you heal my son, I will give my life to you."

Mother used to put one week's supply of phenobarbital in a pill bottle and replenish it weekly so she could make sure I was taking my seizure controlling medicine as directed. A few weeks after Woody and Mallie returned from Washington, Woody came up to my room to pray for my healing. His prayer was short and to the point. After finishing, he pointed at the pill bottle on top of my dresser and said that I did not need to take those anymore. I was pretty much oblivious as to what the pills were for and was happy to oblige. As was her custom, a few days later mother came to replenish my pills at the end of the week to find that several of them were still there. She chided me for not taking my medicine, but for the first time in my life I had a valid excuse for disobedience. Off she went to find Woody. Woody explained that he had prayed for me as directed in the book of James 5 and that he believed I was healed. He said that since there were no elders in their church who would anoint me with oil and believe for my healing, as the elder of the home, he resolved to handle it himself. My mother said that was fine but that my new condition would need to be verified by a doctor before she would take me off the meds.

My mother believed that God could heal me, but she had her doubts about it coming through Woody. She knew he had sold out to Jesus, but it was hard to imagine a miracle coming through him, considering his past. If a "holy man" such as a healing evangelist or even a preacher had prayed for me it would have been much more believable. Nevertheless, she took me back to the doctor. I had the same EEG, in the same hospital, read by the same doctor—only this time with very different results. There were no signs of epilepsy. I was well and today, as a forty seven year old, have not had a seizure since.

God used my healing to draw my mother to Him. She made a deal and was now fully onboard. No longer would God have just a place in my parents' lives. He was *first* place. They wanted to know God intimately and began seeking Him with all their hearts. With my healing fresh on their minds, they tuned in more and more to religious TV programming that gave God more credit than what was offered in traditional main street doctrine. For a family vacation, we all loaded into our yellow station wagon with brown wood paneling and drove to Fort Worth, Texas to a Kenneth

Copeland Crusade. When my parents decided to push the envelope by discussing these biblically based, but denominationally unapproved, teachings in their church, they quickly learned about the "left foot of fellowship" as they were asked to leave. They soon found a "full gospel" church in Tuscaloosa where they would continue to grow in the faith.

At this time I was still a very sick boy. Even though there wasn't any more concern that I might suffer from a random seizure, my heart was broken. My paternal father had recently died, but no clear reason was provided for his death. I was told his lungs collapsed, but the reason smelled fishy, even to an eleven year old. An even more painful question was: Why didn't I know what he looked like? He never visited. I have vague memories of playing catch with a faceless man that I think was my father, but I cannot be sure it was him. I also have fond memories of him driving me to the top of a mountain where he bought me a rubber alligator at the gift shop. I somehow begged him out of some hiking boots, and he stopped on the side of the road so we could scale one of the rocky hillsides. Except for a few pictures, I would not have a clue as to his appearance today. I remember, when I was eight, being told that he would be coming to visit. I excitedly rode my skateboard lap after lap around my mom's car in the driveway, waiting for him to show up, but he never came. I had been to see my father's parents, Pete and Sassie Givhan, from time to time. During one of the visits to my grandparents, I remember they got my father on the phone for a very awkward and brief conversation.

He sounded so nice, intelligent, and like he genuinely cared about me, but that was the only time I can say for sure that I spoke with him. In 1979, my sister and I attended his funeral in Montevallo, AL. A lot of my father's family and friends were there, but I scarcely knew them either. Francis Peterson Givhan, Jr. died at thirty-six.

No two people could be more different than me and my stepfather. Not to mention our personalities, he was a 300 pound chunk of a man, and I was tall and very skinny. Things were acceptable until he and mother had a boy and girl of their own not long after marriage. I am convinced that no matter how hard a stepparent tries, it is impossible to treat a child and stepchild equally, such that the stepchild won't notice. I soon got jealous and started aggravating the younger ones and brought down the wrath of Woody on my head quite often. No matter how hard he tried, he was not my father, and nobody else would do. Nobody ever mentioned my paternal father in the Browder household, but when my mind went there it was never pleasant.

Shortly after returning from the Kenneth Copeland Crusade in Fort Worth, I was upstairs in my room thinking about my father and asking a lot of questions. The result was that I wound up laying on my bed in the fetal position, sobbing and crying. When I got myself together, I noticed and began to read a booklet I snagged in Fort Worth by Pastor Jerry Savelle. I then had my first "God Moment." The message was that God loved me, that He was my real Father, and that He would never leave or forsake me.

My heart was instantly healed. From that point forward, I would have a peace and assurance that comes only from the one who formed me in my mother's womb. My obnoxious treatment of others dissipated. I even remember overhearing my peers at school saying that I had changed. God separated me from all dependence on my earthly father so that I would become keenly dependent on Him at an early age.

The Revelation

Years later, as a senior in high school, while rummaging through mom's overflowing and seldom used china cabinet drawers, a very interesting discovery was made. I found a card that was written to my mother expressing sympathy for the death of my father. The card referred to his "sickness." I showed it to my sister and we decided to confront mother for answers. When we did, a look of solemnity came over her face as she braced herself. After all these years she finally revealed that our father was mentally ill. He was diagnosed as a paranoid schizophrenic. A flood of emotions came crashing down on us that day. My sister withdrew to her room upset and crying. My mind was racing in many different directions. At first, I was relieved that he was sick. At least it helped me justify his absence. Finally, it was all starting to make sense. I recalled all the strange looks from those attending his funeral. I was the crazy dead man's son and maybe I was, or would be, just a crazy as he was. I knew what they were thinking because I was wondering the same thing. *Was I crazy? If not now, would I be?* And now I knew why there was no discussion about my father, or if there was it was awk-ward.

The whole matter had been top secret. My mother was no doubt traumatized by her experiences with my father and had great difficulty discussing any of it. Moreover, she would not want the stigma of mental illness attached to me or my sister. For these reasons, she would not discuss the situation with anyone. My father's family would certainly keep it as quiet as possible. My Givhan grandparents knew a lot more than they were telling. They knew something was wrong with my father early on but chose to keep my mother in the dark as she followed their disturbed son here and there as his mental illness took hold.

The Givhan name was worth protecting. As far as southern aristocracy went, few families have better credentials. My Givhan ancestry traces back to the border between Germany and France who were most likely French Huguenots that fled Europe due to religious persecution. The "h" in Givhan is silent and some suppose it was inserted as a secret sign indicating them as Huguenots. Once in America, my ancestors settled in South Carolina, acquired land, slaves and farmed as long as cotton was king. When their soil was depleted, they marched westward through the generations in search of fertile ground. When the Civil War put an end to the program, they had gotten as far as Alabama. After the war, my forefathers gravitated toward the practice of medicine. My father's older brother Edgar Givhan, MD was no exception. He was a well-respected author and hematologist. My father's sister, Gene, had no history of mental illness. What happened to father was a mystery and I had a lot of questions for which there were not any clear answers. Answers were coming, but it would be years later before more pieces of the puzzle would fall into place.

Veneer Milling

Before I graduated from college, I decided to legally change my name by adding my stepfather's last name to mine. I became Francis Peterson Givhan Browder. Woody had been asking my mother to change my last name to his for years, but mother had resisted, as she knew how prestigious the Givhan name was. She used to say that it was the only thing of value that I had gotten from my father. When I became of age as an adult, I took matters into my own hands and chose to do it myself in appreciation for all that Woody had done for me.

In 1991, I graduated from Alabama with a degree in English, married my girlfriend, Chris, and went to work for my stepfather. Woody was against the marriage from the beginning and refused to smile in any of the wedding pictures. My new bride became our only office staff and performed all the necessary tasks of making payroll, paying bills, and invoicing. I called myself working for Woody all through high school and by the time I finished college I knew my way around the mill pretty well. Making a living in the veneer business was far from glamorous. It was long hours of hard work in either hot or cold weather, dealing with laborers who worked there only because they had no other choice. I never knew what my day would bring or if I would ever get any time off work. I was always on call and feeling the pressure of the responsibility. We had contractors to help with bigger projects, but on a daily basis I wore the hats of a salesman, HR manager, welder, machine operator, and whatever else it took to get product out the door on time and according to specification.

Chris made a beautiful bride. Anything but slight of frame, she was naturally well-built and curvy in all the right places. She was tenderhearted with an infectious, affectionate, and bubbly personality. Deep down inside, her heart was damaged by her parents' divorce when she was very young. She was raised by her mother but did not have a close relationship with either parent. It was clear that Chris was hoping to be folded into my family as a daughter to fill the void of her dysfunctional family experience.

Eutaw was not the best of places to live for a young couple. Chris seemed to feed off the approval of others. The tiny population was very cliquish, gossipy, and judgmental. My marriage was deeply strained by the fact that Woody made no effort to hide his disapproval of my marriage. The situation proved unbearable to my wife. As the pressure mounted, she talked to me about her concerns. I was shocked that she was contemplating divorce because there hadn't been any major drama between the two of us. Her motives became clear when she asked if I thought we would ever live anywhere else. I loved her deeply but could not bear the thought that her commitment to me was based on such shallow conditions. After thinking about it, I fought back the urge to appease her unfounded feelings for me. I told her that I would never leave Eutaw. After 11 months of marriage, she was gone, and we had a quick, uncontested divorce and I was left all alone wondering what had happened. I could not believe that this had happened to me. Other than Woody's disapproval, there was nothing to indicate a struggle between us. There hadn't been any warning signs, and I came to the realization that to her our relationship was nothing more than a stepping stone to a better destination. I could not believe that her love for me was so insincere. I knew that Woody had deeply wounded her, but if that was all it took to cancel her feelings for me, then he was right. I should not have married her. We had been married such a short time that we should have been still "honeymooning." Much to my surprise, she was gone and a flood of emotions jockeyed for control. Feelings of loneliness, rejection, and failure instantly descended upon me and filled my head like a fog that refused to dissipate.

Woody was a very demanding boss. He was a micro-manager and had be in control of every little detail. That being said, he was very successful and I was amazed at how profitable his little business was. Somehow Woody had taken his father's company that went bankrupt during Jimmy Carter's term, paid off all the debt and was printing money. Interestingly, the good times did not come until after he gave his life to God, got sober, and married my mom.

Business was very good in the 90's. Most of our veneers were sold to office chair manufacturers. We had one primary customer, The Hon Company, who consumed nearly all our production. It was a very scary prospect, considering our dependence on one customer, but it was also a chance to further increase profitability by customizing and streamlining our production. Young and energetic, I encouraged Woody to update our residual waste handling equipment that resulted in tremendous efficiency improvements. Our sales of both veneer and wood chips went up by 20%. Woody was thrilled because he was soon knocking down a million dollars a year profit.

With new found affluence, and me living in Eutaw taking care of the business, Woody decided to move to Tuscaloosa so his younger kids would have better opportunities. He would still come down to work most days, but I did my best to handle everything his way so he could do as he pleased. I had been his apprentice for years and could accurately guess how he would handle most any situation. A quick-tempered type, it was best to keep him out of the mill as much as possible anyway to avoid disrupting the staff. Woody was so pleased with my handling of things that he gave me thirty percent ownership of the company. I was touched deeply by his gesture and became all the more loyal and as I was making several hundred thousand dollars per year.

The only problem was that I was lonely and tied down to the job. I found out the hard way that Eutaw, Alabama is a very hard place for young couples to survive. Single people have very few options, and I decided to move to Tuscaloosa where I bought the ultimate bachelor pad, situated on the Black Warrior River directly across from the university. The location was awesome. I could be anywhere in town within minutes and sit on my back porch listening to roars in Bryant-Denny Stadium during football season. Even though I had a 40 minute commute to work, it was well worth it. The sting of my failed marriage soon became nothing more than an easily blocked out memory as I reconnected with friends and would soon have the semblance of a life outside of work. My memories were forced to the surface when my ex-wife dropped by unannounced. I had no interest in a rekindling any sort of relationship with her, but I invited her in and enjoyed showing her my new pad, which was not in Eutaw. I was nice to her, but to be honest I was hoping that she regretted leaving me and if so, then what would it hurt to rub it in a little? She had her chance, and it was too late for her. Besides, I was no longer attracted to her, and she was much older than the ladies I had grown accustomed to checking out. As a UA alumnus, I got a pass to exercise at the UA recreation center with my friends and it felt like I was still in college on the weekends.

My life as a single man was short-lived. In 1995, I was set up on a blind date with a dark-haired beauty named Audra. The moment I saw her, I recognized her from having seen her face around the fraternity house on dates with another brother. We immediately hit it off. Audra worked for her father and understood the demands of family business. Woody and her mom were college acquaintances and he immediately endorsed and encouraged the relationship. After a quick courtship, we were married in March of 1996. Our marriage would be the first of a fast-paced chain of events that would dramatically change our lives. Other than my house, I didn't have any debt. Most of what I made, I saved. We sold her house and she moved into mine. My first chore was to pay off her credit cards and even an armoire she had financed. With two incomes and a modicum of financial discipline, money quickly became a non-issue.

After a few months of marriage, Audra came to understand the magnitude of the weight that I carried at work. It was not that the job was so difficult. The issue was that there was hardly ever a break from it. The only way to relieve the pressure was for the mill to be down. When we closed for holidays, it was time for major maintenance projects that required my supervision. If I was gone, it meant Woody had to step up and the mechanical aspects of the business were not his forte. To get a week off for our honeymoon took an act of congress, and his poor attitude toward giving me time off was quickly noted by my new wife. This did not sit well with her, and we soon came to resent the situation. Having learned lessons from my first failed marriage, I was very sensitive to my wife's complaints and resolved to protect my marriage by making her my priority. Unlike before, I was ready to defend my marriage at the expense of my job if necessary.

In the summer of 1996, I saw a brochure on Woody's desk advertising the sale of a veneer mill in Centreville, AL. Both Woody and I lived in Tuscaloosa. Eutaw was 30 miles to the West and Centreville was 30 miles to the East of Tuscaloosa. The mill in Centreville was owned by Mannington Wood Floors. Mannington had recently built a state of the art mill in Epes, AL and wanted to divest of their older mill in Centreville. Immediately I got excited with the prospect of growing our business to include another location. To me it seemed like a great idea to have two mills. My younger brother was in college and said he wanted to work in the family business after graduation. Even though he was 10 years younger, he was Woody's flesh and blood and I figured there would be conflict if I were boss over him. As far as I was concerned, there would be resentment on my part if I were not. Even as boss, I would not be happy if I did all the heavy lifting while he sat back and collected a big paycheck. I am not sure why I was the only one who saw this coming. After all, the same situation went down between Woody and his younger brother and I wanted nothing to do with that sort of strife. On top of that, I was bored with the mill we had and wanted to expand into other markets, but Woody would have none of it.

Woody and I discussed buying the other mill, and he said he was considering it. A few days later, he explained his decision to decline—he didn't have any debt and at his age he did not want to risk the good thing he had going. I told him I understood his feelings and asked if he minded if I looked at buying it myself. He gave me his blessing.

From that day forward, I had a new swing in my step. All the troubles I foresaw in the family business could be averted. The thought of owning my own business simply thrilled me. I wanted to be just like Woody. I envisioned making tons of money and the freedom to live my life unencumbered by the daily grind. If my wife wanted to go on vacation, I was the boss. No problem. If I wanted to play golf during the week, I was the boss. No problem.

I discussed the opportunity with my wife. She was equally ambitious and supported the idea. Working for Woody was no joke, and by this time, Audra had gotten a good taste of how controlling he was. This was our way out. Immediately, she connected me with the accounting firm, Jamison, Money and Farmer who did work for her father. One of the largest and well-thought of firms in Tuscaloosa, JMF provided mergers and acquisitions services. I was introduced to a remarkably talented deal maker named Charlie Horton. Charlie was the grizzled, gray-haired veteran who handled complex transactions such as the purchase and sale of businesses.

After a few meetings, Charlie and his assistants thoroughly dissected every important aspect of the opportunity. One of the first questions they had was how much money did I have. I was 27 years old and had saved about two hundred thousand dollars, which was a mere ten percent of the purchase price. With all the information in hand, Charlie went to work. Millions of dollars would have to be borrowed to swing the deal. The only borrowing experience I had was buying a house, so I did not know the standards of business loans. Charlie knew banks would not take this risk without more security, but he did not share with me how slim the chances were of getting our deal done. Charlie searched for government-backed loans for small businesses. He looked at both

Small Business Administration (SBA) and Federal Housing Administration (FHA) options. The SBA option was not a fit, but the FHA had a loan guarantee program for small businesses in rural areas and it looked like our purchase checked all the boxes. Charlie put together bid packages to the larger banks around town in an attempt to elicit offers.

As Charlie worked out the kinks of the acquisition, months had gone by since Woody had given me his consent to pursue the purchase. While I continued to explore the possibility of the purchase, Woody got more and more irritable by the day. Woody had not been straight with me. He was adamantly against me buying the mill and leaving him from the start. It would be ten years before my mother told me the truth. Early on, Woody had been consoled by his banker, Victor Poole, who told him not to worry about me leaving because there was no way that a bank would lend me that kind of money. With that in mind, he decided to play it cool, tell me to go for it, and just let it play out. When it did not resolve as quickly as he imagined, he got increasingly angry with me but never told me how he really felt.

All this time I was performing my duties at work as usual and never discussed it with him, but he knew what was going on because I would get occasional phone calls from those working on the acquisition. In the fall of 1996, Woody could not handle it anymore. I was out in the plant working when he came up to me and started yelling at me for no good reason. I told him to kiss my ass and that was the last day I would ever work at Sumter Veneer.

My wife was in shock. After all, I was doing quite well eight months prior when we married, but now I was unemployed. Yes, there was the prospect of the new mill, but that was far from a done deal. Looking into the option to buy the mill seemed like a good idea as long as it did not result in the loss of my current job but unfortunately that was exactly what happened.

There was not much I could do to facilitate the purchase, even though thoughts of it consumed me day and night. I began piddling around my father-in-law's business to keep busy, but it was a very strange feeling to be unemployed. One of the worst aspects of the situation was the wrath of Woody as it pertained to my relationships with the rest of the family. I immediately became a black sheep and nobody even called to get my side of the story except my mother. During this time, Woody made her life miserable and I felt horrible for being the cause of it.

After about a month of being unemployed, I got news that of all the banks solicited, there were only two that were possibly interested. Southtrust was one of them and we were overjoyed when the local president asked Audra and me to meet with them at Cypress Inn restaurant to discuss our plans. The meeting would not go so well. Audra's father was a client of Southtrust and the venue was nothing more than an attempt to gently explain their refusal, and furthermore that no other bank would view it differently. Audra was livid, as she could not believe they would ask us to dinner only to dash our hopes.

At this point, Amsouth Bank was our only hope. The commercial loan department of Amsouth in Tuscaloosa was run by an industrious banker named Kevin McMahon. Unlike other bankers in the area who had refused our deal, Kevin was not too lazy to work through the red tape of the Federal government to apply for a FHA loan guaranty. As it turned out, Kevin got FHA approval and received the support of Amsouth hierarchy to make me an offer. Thankfully, I had a very rich uncle named Sam who would co-sign with me and promise to pay up to ninety percent of the loan should it default.

Shortly after getting the good news, my mother called to arrange a visit. There was something very urgent that she needed to discuss with me. I had not seen her much since the falling out and from the moment I saw her, I knew she had been under great stress. Woody had been put back to work full-time and nobody would feel the pain of that transition more than she would. Not only was he back at work, but he also was faced with the complication that he had become hostile with someone who owned 30% of his company and knew all his business. I knew Woody had not been playing fair with me as a stockholder, but I never said anything because I felt it was not my place in light of the fact that what ownership I had he had given to me. Even though I was a shareholder, he easily manipulated how much he would share with me by adjusting his salary—his payroll check had gotten very large. If any profit accumulated, he would then distribute it 70/30 between us at his sole discretion. By this time, Woody's accountant was sure to have shared with him the seriousness of his dilemma. Since the day we parted, no distributions were made to me, and I felt sure that Woody had seen to it that there were no profits to distribute. I also knew that a mean lawyer could fix that.

Mother and I met for lunch. The main reason for our visit was that she had been sent to negotiate for the return of my company stock and offer me a distribution check that was supposed to represent 30% of profits since my departure and would be the last one I would ever receive. I took the check and discussed it with my wife. We were happy to have the surprise funding, considering the mill purchase was sucking me dry. However, it was quite the dilemma to give up my stock considering the obligations I would soon have. As I was gathering courage to do the right thing, the attorney who was handling the mill purchase adamantly objected to the return of the shares. This was the first time that I saw first-hand just how bad advice from attorneys could be. There was no way that I would be a part of dishonoring my parents by refusing to honor their wishes. Yes, I told my stepfather to kiss my ass, but he had been good to me, and I held no grudge against him even if I could not work for him anymore. The stock was given to me with the understanding that I would be there to run the mill, and I had walked away. I gave my shares of Sumter Veneer stock to my younger brother as requested.

Mother's Gift

I had always been close to my mother, and nothing would ever change that. After she offered to give her life to God in exchange for my healing that day on the train, God did his part and she held up her end. I have never known anyone who loves God more than she does. Though I am admittedly partial, I am not just saying that because she is my mother. She truly is a very special and gifted woman of God. Rarely does she do anything that she is not in prayer. No matter what task she does around the house it seems she is always talking to God. She reads her Bible relentlessly and seems to worship God constantly. I did not fully appreciate her spiritual gifts as I should have, but from time to time I would catch a glimpse of God working through her and her gifting.

At this time of my life, I was singularly focused on my new wife and veneer mill that I hoped would meet all my expectations. I was trusting God through it all, but in my mind He was mainly there to serve me. 1996 was a big year for me. I got married in March, quit my job in September, and on my twenty-eighth birthday on November 19, 1996, I received a present from God, written by my mother.

Pete –

For your birthday: God has a special message for you. He loves you very much. When you were very young I chose you as my very own. Now that you are grown and have many responsibilities you are much of my concern. Don't ever despair and think I'm not there. I'm always here for you. I rejoice in your thankfulness. I have great pleasure in your needing me. I stand by your side in all your needs. I love you very much my son. Rejoice and give thanks for about what I am doing in your life. Praise Father, Son and Holy Ghost. Let your light shine. Forgiveness is a fruit I want to give to you. This fruit makes everything sweet in your life. When you give it away – it sets you free. Praise Father, Son and Holy Ghost. Whisper into my ear your every fear. I will wipe them away. Shine like I want you to with the brightness of my love. Never be a people pleaser. Only try to please me. I'm really the only one that counts. Your will should be changed to my will. I desire to bless you. I desire to make you an overcomer. I desire your respect. I need you and want you as my own. Pray for the God of harvest to bring in many souls. You will help minister unto them. You are a chosen vessel. Rise high, soar high above the problems of life. Always give them to me and I will take care of them. You are a Priesthood, a royal nation. I plan to show you great and marvelous things.

So be it—

When I read the words for the first time, I was stunned and just stared. The whole message was surreal, but I never doubted its authenticity. It was all good, but it seemed like God was talking to someone else in much of it. I was about to buy a veneer business with a hundred employees and had no intent to be any sort of minister or preacher. I remembered how my mother had made a similar statement, 17 years prior, at about the same time that I got healed of epilepsy. She told me that I was going to be a minister one day and I told her that I would never do that. How was that possible considering the path I was on? I could not make sense of it. What did He mean by fruit of forgiveness and setting me free when I gave it away? I wondered what marvelous things He would show me. Thirteen years would go by before I finally had a grasp of the meaning of these words, but every one of them would come to pass exactly as written. For the time being, it would suffice that the same God who was there for me as a broken hearted boy continued to reveal himself, and that I could count on Him.

The encouragement was just in time because on February 24, 1997, I would become the sole owner of Cahaba Veneer, Inc., and just like that I was three million dollars in debt. The purchase of the property was only part of the debt I would acquire. I had to borrow a lot more to finance working capital and inventory. I only thought I had a lot of pressure on me while working for Woody. The fantasy of what I thought it would be like as a mill owner quickly turned into a nightmare. I soon realized that much of the mill equipment was in very poor condition and in need of repairs or replacement. Cahaba Veneer was three times the size of Sumter Veneer with enhanced capabilities, but it took 5 times as many people to operate. Profit margins were slim and what profits were generated in excess of loan payments had to be spent on equipment and infrastructure improvements. I soon realized that I had taken for granted much of what Woody had accomplished and the load he carried. He had key business relationships in place that had taken many years to develop. I would not ride the coattails of any of those relationships because I was treated as a traitor that none of them were willing to partner with. This would be no easy task for me, so I worked very long days. My hopes of having an improved personal life and marriage as a result of being an owner were dashed and set aside. I was driven to prove myself and would die trying if that was what it took.

A few weeks after closing on the mill, another shocking revelation came. Audra was pregnant. We were thinking of starting a family sometime in the near future but not quite that soon. We had been married barely a year, and in that time I lost my job, spent all our money, was deep in debt, was working long hours struggling to make a new business fly and now she was pregnant!? I was surprised but also thrilled as I considered how much my life had changed in such a short period of time. Surely things would settle down soon.

A few months into pregnancy, I managed to tear myself away from work to go to an ultrasound appointment to see our baby. Everything was going great as the technician helped us identify features of our healthy child. Suddenly the tech sat up and muttered something under her breath. She then asked us if we knew we were having twins. Audra gasped, and instantly beads of sweat formed on her forehead. In disbelief, I practically ran to the other side of the bed, which was closer to the monitor, demanding to see proof. The tech continued to move the wand over Audra's belly, pointing at the screen which revealed various features of two children in her womb. There they were, we were having twin daughters and our world was rocked again.

Audra recovered a few moments after the placement of a cold wash cloth across her forehead. The ride home was strangely quiet as we stared blankly into space, wondering what laid in store for us. Audra grew so big, so fast that I could hardly believe my eyes, and I was buying Nutter Butters by the case.

On December 11, 1997, I was the proud father of identical twin daughters, Carley Ruth and Carey Frances. From that point forward, life would be very different but more so for Audra than for me. As a child, she was into riding horses as opposed to dolls or baby-sitting. As an adult, she was the professional, career-minded type who was nowhere close to being ready for one on each hip. In preparation of being a new mother, Audra set aside her duties at work, but she had to have help. My cousin Amy helped us for a while and gave us much needed relief during the day but at night there was symphony of cries as both girls had bouts of colic that would go on for months. Amy told us upfront that she could only help short-term. Long before we were ready, I had to find someone else. Willie Ann Murphy was an employee at the mill, and I heard she had experience in this line of work. I quickly asked her if she was interested in helping us at home. I thank God that she agreed to show up at our house at 8:00 AM and work until 5:00 PM Monday through Friday and even Saturdays if we wanted. She would even go with us on vacations if we asked her to. With everything we were juggling, it was still a very difficult time, but with Willie Ann's help, we could make it.

For me, the next few years were a blur. My business venture had not turned out exactly as planned, but Cahaba Veneer made money every year, even if nearly all of it had to be used to service debt and update or replace equipment. By year 2000, huge changes came to our customer base. Furniture manufacturing was being outsourced to Asia at an alarming rate. In 1997, about 75% of Cahaba Veneer products were sold to clients who further processed them into furniture and the rest into engineered wood flooring. Within a few short years of buying the mill, most of the US furniture manufacturing plants would be closed. China had opened its doors and the highly skilled, low wage Chinese labor was a temptation that Western business could not resist.

Veneer mills in the south have traditionally produced a lower grade veneer which was hidden in various furniture products. The veneers could be pressed into structural plywood parts of various shapes and contours but were often buried beneath layers of foam and fabric. These low-end veneers could be produced with relatively loose quality standards and customers rarely complained. When furniture orders died, the only other viable option was the engineered flooring business. Engineered flooring is hardwood plywood (wood veneers glued together) that is sawn into flooring planks. Engineered flooring customers were much more demanding than furniture customers. They had to be because their products were exposed and closely inspected by end users every day for many years. These companies had rigorous quality control audits of every shipment they received and they tracked every vendor's material all the way through their factories.

Making the transition to flooring would not be easy, but the timing could not have been better. Popularity of engineered flooring was increasing as was demand for the raw veneers needed to manufacture it. Wood flooring manufacturers would closely consider taking their production overseas but by and large did not because the labor component of flooring costs are much lower than that of furniture. Wood flooring production could be highly automated and the numbers did not support a move to China. The writing was on the wall. It was time to step up our game and focus on wood flooring.

With all this activity, I was distracted from what was going on around my house. Willie Ann was showing up every day for work and Audra had since quit her job to do pretty much whatever she wanted as long as Willie was there to help her with the kids. I strayed from my original goals of putting my family first. I thought I had everything situated so I could be where I was needed most. The mill was my baby and it needed lots of personal care. In my mind it had to come first because from it flowed the rest of our sustenance. I did not realize the problems that this improper ordering of priorities was causing. My wife and I were drifting further and further apart and would soon be in dangerous territory.

In 2002, the mill was nearly paid for. A wealthy attorney friend of our family had recently built a magnificent home north of town but was now moving to another city. I started thinking about selling our river front home and buying their house which was tucked into a cul-de-sac of one of the most affluent neighborhoods in town. At 8,000 square feet it was way more home than we would ever need, but I was intrigued and thought it would be a good investment. I was driven to demonstrate my success and manhood by providing material things for my family at an impressive level. That was my identity. This new home was further from work, but that was just another way I could show how much I was willing to sacrifice for my wife and kids. One thing led to another and we sold our riverfront home for a tidy profit and parlayed it into the monster home that cost well over a million dollars.

To begin with, Audra was a little hesitant to agree with my desire to move into this large house. There was nothing wrong with what we had, but she ultimately changed her tune. For over a year she thought of nothing other than furniture and decor. We agreed on a sizable budget, and off she went. She hired a professional designer from Birmingham who charged ridiculous rates for her advice and draperies. Audra drug me off to Baton Rouge to an antique store just to buy a fancy gold framed mirror to go over the mantle. I knew she would spend a lot of money furnishing the house—but she had lost her mind! When I realized that she had spent over two hundred thousand dollars, I shut her down. Much to my dismay, pretty much every room in the house was done up to the hilt except the one I cared about the most, the master bedroom.

At this time the mill was doing so well that I hardly missed the money. The transition to flooring was paying off. Cahaba Veneer could produce larger sizes than many of our competitors which allowed us to sell some of our products with better margins. The mills that needed these larger sizes developed close partnerships with us. In 2002, the buyer for the largest engineered manufacturer in the US called and said that their sales projections were off the chart. He promised that he would take double what I currently produced and he urged me to do whatever necessary to meet his needs. He could not offer me a written contract but he gave me his word that he would see to it that I would be taken care of as long as they needed veneer.

I remember discussing this opportunity with Audra just as we were settling into our new house. The mill was almost paid for then and I was suggesting that we borrow millions more to expand and meet the needs of our customers. As ambitious as she was, she was not thrilled with the idea—but I would not be dissuaded. At last, she reluctantly gave me her support.

I was confident that God's blessing was on our lives and that I could not lose. Throughout my life, miracle after miracle had taken place to support my belief and as far as I was concerned there was nothing to it but to do it. For the next few years, I spent about three million dollars modernizing and expanding the mill. The project demanded much of my time and I enjoyed every minute of it, but my relationship with my wife suffered greatly.

In hindsight, it is hard to believe just how much my goals changed after I became a business owner. Many of the things I loathed about working for Woody were not only acceptable but fully embraced now that I owned my own business. I thought that having my own plant would mean more freedom, but in reality I had become a slave to it. The business was my idol. I chalked it up to duty, but to be successful was my top motivation and nobody or nothing would get in the way of my achieving it. Audra always struggled to get me to commit to a vacation. Most times she would just make plans and hope I would go because there was no good time for me to be away or at least that was what I thought. Not only that, but I also hated dropping thousands of dollars on trips that would be over in a few days all the while poor decisions might be made in my absence costing me even more.

There is one vacation that I will never forget. Arrangements were made to stay with my grandmother who lived on the beach in Gulf Shores, AL. We had this trip planned for several weeks, but my grandmother called at the last minute saying she would be attending the funeral of her sister in New England. She insisted that we come anyway. She was living in a condo at The Beach Club and there was no reason why we could not keep our plans and enjoy it in her absence. During our stay something very strange happened that would be a hint toward the plans God had for me.

A few days into our stay, Audra wakened me in the wee hours of the morning. As the fog receded from my mind, she hurriedly explained that someone had been banging on the door of the condo. She answered it without me and when she cracked the door for conversation, a woman forced her way in and helped herself to an unoccupied bedroom. Audra was completely freaked-out because the twins were sleeping in a bedroom directly across the hall and this person was not in her right mind. As I fumbled to get dressed, I scolded her for opening the door, but she explained that she thought she recognized the person's voice as that of my cousin Suzanna. She further explained that her intent was to crack the door and dismiss her. Once the door was unlocked, Suzanna's entry was so brash and forceful that Audra was visibly shaken.

Taking a deep breath, I gathered my wits and softly knocked on the door to Suzanna's room. I waited but got no answer and carefully opened the door to peek inside. The lights were on and I saw two single beds with barely enough space to walk between them. It was clear that grandmother used this room for storage more than anything else. One of the beds was loaded down with various and sundry things that women who have lived through the Great Depression hoard. On the other laid Suzanna on top of the bed spread on her back fully dressed with shoes on and eyes closed.

I could not remember the last time that I had seen her. She had always been an exceptionally beautiful girl with natural blonde hair, blue eyes, tan skin, and a figure that would draw envy from her peers. About three years younger than me, we grew up spending a lot of time as juveniles in Tuscaloosa. Very outgoing and friendly, Suzanna never met a stranger. Living two blocks from the University of Alabama strip and three blocks from fraternity row meant there was always a party waiting to be crashed anytime she had the urge. Her parents were lax in their supervision and she found it way too easy to sneak out her bedroom window to do as she pleased. At this time she was about 30 years old. Having spent her youth in the fast lane, she was coping with a host of problems which stemmed from a myriad of poor decisions. Suzanna had wholeheartedly embraced a life of pleasure and was now having a very difficult time bringing her vehicle under control. Her brake lines had been somehow cut during her long, strange trip. Sex and drug addictions clung to her relentlessly. If it felt good, she had pursued it without limit, but she knew she was living life on the edge and had to get it under control before there was a fatal crash. As hard as she tried, she was struggling to find freedom from the bondage to which she had unwittingly sold herself. She had come to experience the truth of the wise: Sin would take you farther than you want to go, keep you longer than you wanted to stay, and cost you more than you wanted to pay.

Suzanna was anything but lazy. Despite her issues, she had become a dental hygienist and relocated to the Alabama Gulf Coast. The small strip of Alabama beach was the beginning of the sugar white sand playground that extends eastward through Florida. As premier vacation destinations, these Gulf of Mexico beaches are non-stop party locations from Spring Break through Labor Day. While on vacation, it is understood and expected that even the most conservative of beach goers would be there in hopes getting relief from the ordinary stresses of life. Following the principles of supply and demand, drugs and alcohol are readily available to anyone seeking full release of the tensions of life. I was not surprised that this was Suzanna's choice for permanent residence.

When I opened the door and looked into the room, I called her name, but she never looked up or in any way acknowledged my presence. Perplexed and unsure of her condition, I cleared away enough room on the opposite bed to sit and observe while I pondered what to do. Of course I suspected that she was under the influence of drugs or alcohol. She didn't smell or act like she was drunk, so I assumed that she was high on something else.

I just stared at her in amazement. I had never seen anything like it. She was mumbling to herself, but it was as if there were multiple, rapid fire conversations going on in her head and that individual speakers were taking turns speaking through her mouth. I guess the closest thing that I had ever seen like it was from the late actor Robin Williams. Robin was well known for his ability to demonstrate conversations of various people in quick-witted comedic episodes. The main difference was that what she said did not make sense. It was as if there were many conversations going on in her head and she was jumping from one to another. After listening for a few minutes, I wondered if these were the discussions of demons and if they would answer me if addressed. I asked, "What is your name?" Immediately the muttering stopped and words came from her mouth that shocked me. "We are many." My mind raced as I remembered the response of Legion to Jesus from the Gadarene demoniac. Before I could respond, the demon called me a fool, and the muttering started again. A fool? I wondered what the demon knew about me. I tried to interrupt with more questions but was ignored.

I was in no way prepared to challenge demons, but they were right there inside my cousin, who I loved and wanted to help. This was no small deal because she was out of her mind and in close proximity to my wife and five year old daughters. My prayer life was practically non-existent, but prayer was the only thing I could think of doing. When I dropped my head to pray, Suzanna instantly snapped out of it. I barely said "Dear Lord" before she looked at me and affectionately exclaimed, "Peterson, what are you doing here? Umm, what am I doing here?" In an instant she was completely lucid and coherent with no sign of any debility. Her transformation also resulted in a loving greeting and smiles that were consistent with her normal personality. There was no doubt that she was under the influence, but it was clear that the greatest influence would not register on any drug or alcohol tests. She seemed to have a vague recollection of what had transpired that evening. She recounted having a few drinks with her husband at The Beach Club bar which ended in a fight, but after that it was all a blur. With compassion, I filled her in on what I knew and my conversation with what I thought were her demons. Though upsetting, I could tell this was not news to her and that her distress came more from me knowing. I prayed for her and agreed to drive her home. Five miles later we pulled up to her house. She did not have a purse or keys and she was locked out. I sat in my vehicle as the sun began to rise watching her check the windows and doors of her home. She returned to say that her husband had hidden his vehicle around back in hopes she would think he was not there. She would not be fooled and for the second time in one night would pound on a door until it opened.

As concerned as I was for my cousin, I had no clue about what I could do for her and had no choice but to leave her in that condition. The next Sunday I shared the story with my Sunday school class at Calvary Baptist in Tuscaloosa. Everyone was intrigued, but they were all just as ignorant as I was about what could be done. Suzanna would regularly come into my mind for years after that experience as I wondered how she was and what I might do to help her.

The Beginning of the End

There is nothing worse than living with someone who has become a complete stranger. Working long hours and commuting about an hour each way, I was out early and in late sacrificing for the team. It had been my ambition to provide for my family in ways that few could boast. In exchange, my ego demanded occasional attention, appreciation, and respect. My pride would not allow anything less.

A major turning point in my marriage was the night that Audra coldly turned down my advances. From that point forward, it was as if a switch flipped deep inside my heart. The fact that I would not be having sex was not what got to me. There was nothing unusual about being rebuffed, but in times past she had at least pretended to be concerned about my needs and would tenderly ask for a raincheck when, for whatever the reason, my timing was not right or too frequent. This night all I got was an aloof, cold hearted response that sent me reeling and stung me to the core. Immediately I hopped out of bed, announcing that it was alright and that I would find some somewhere else as I marched to the bedroom across the hall. I did not mean it, nor did I have desire for anyone else. My intent was to use harsh words in a last ditch effort to elicit some sort of pulse from her hardened heart, but all she did was completely ignore my threat. A few minutes later, to my utter dismay, she further punctuated her lack of concern for my feelings with a cacophony of snoring. Something came over me that night, the depths of which would take me years to fully understand. As a general rule, I find it easy to forgive, but this offense was unacceptable, and I decided to hold onto it and make her pay.

Though I should have been tired from a long day's work, my mind raced to heightened levels of alertness and irritation. I recounted how good I was to her and yet she had the nerve to treat me with such contempt. I had been a faithful husband and had no desire to be otherwise. How dare she?! I would show her that I would not be taken advantage of. She was not the only one with stuff that could be withheld. I had spoiled her with my money, and it had been my pleasure to do so, but now it was time to show her how it felt to be coldly cut off.

Anytime I was tempted to think of divorcing my wife, I would quickly set such thoughts aside because of our children. I had needs that my wife had now decided she had no obligation or concern to meet, but I could not entertain abandoning our children considering what I had been through as a child. Having twins meant there was nothing I did not help with. Having a kid means work and twins meant double and double fast. Their development seemed to accelerate as they learned from and competed with one another. If one was crying, the other would cry a little louder. It was quite the experience. From late night feedings, to changing diapers, to playing in the floor or chasing them around the house—I am not saying that I was Mr. Mom, but I did a lot, and if you put Willie Ann in my column then I did the most. Audra and I had completely different ideas of how to raise children. She seemed to believe that the way to make them happy was to give them whatever they wanted, while I was the disciplinarian. She doted on them enough for 10 mothers, and I was concerned that they were getting spoiled. I believed the girls needed me and my perspective to cut through the thick coddling instincts that were skewing the perspective of their mother. The girls were older now, but they needed me, and most importantly they needed to know that I loved them. I was not going anywhere. Even still, Audra needed to be taught a lesson for her unfaithful treatment of me.

If only I knew then what I know now, untold pain and suffering could have been averted. I was ignorant of the trap I had fallen headlong into. I rarely read my Bible and was unprepared for the spiritual battle that I unknowingly was a part of.

Move and Counter Move

The game of chess had begun. I was convinced that Audra did not love me anymore, and I might as well have been an ATM because all she was doing was pushing my buttons and taking my money. If she thought she could use me without consequence, then she had another thing coming, and I would show her a thing or two. Immediately I tightened the purse strings. I told her that she was spending too much money and demanded that she develop and put herself on a budget. I took away her company credit card that she charged her gasoline on. When she repeatedly went over the amount I told her she could spend on my personal card, I cancelled her card and told her to get one in her name. I wanted to hear her squeal and honestly enjoyed seeing her squirm under my new financial policies.

The implementation of austerity measures did not work except to tick her off more. Instead of causing her to appreciate me, she just resented me all the more and found new ways to retaliate. Audra has always been a scrapper and would not be pushed around. Instead of paying necessary bills like our house payment, she blew her monthly allowance on incidentals and demanded more for the necessary bills. When I reduced the amount I gave her and paid the mandatory bills myself, she found new ways to hurt me. She decided to get the girls involved in horse riding. They had to have their own horses. Horses had to be boarded and shoed. Pretty soon she and the girls were sitting in a pasture somewhere around

West Alabama every weekend. The only weekend time with my family was to follow them to some dusty dung strewn riding ring where people loiter around all day in preparation for their child to compete for five minutes. If I went, I just felt out of place as I stood around wondering what I was doing there while she socialized with the other horse moms. Horse riding is a wholesome activity. The girls really enjoyed and excelled at it, but it was consuming most of the time that I normally spent with my family on weekends. Audra dictated their activities, and I had little say over their plans. For that reason, I grew to loathe it. Thoughts began to cross my mind that I would have more time to spend with my kids if we were divorced. At least then they would be with me every other weekend. During this time I became more and more lonely and distant from my wife. Sleeping in separate beds had become the norm as our love grew colder and colder.

The cold war escalated for several years until reaching a breaking point in 2006. 2006 had been a record-breaking year in terms of profitability for my company which contrasted greatly with my loathsome personal life. Even though I was not getting much of anything that I wanted from my marital relationship, Audra had no shame in demanding that she be kept up as in times past. She demanded a new car. I resisted and continued to put the squeeze on her financially. She and I had a joint brokerage account with several hundred thousand dollars invested. We agreed to split it so that we could spend it however we wanted. With her new found wealth, she went out and bought a new BMW and horse trailer. I put mine back into the company.

Just a few miles from the mill, I noticed a unique piece of property was for sale. It was kind of a mini-farm with a few small ponds, a workshop, and a tiny house up on a hill overlooking a hundred acres. The house was unattractive, small and very strange, but the land was private and had a captivating view. The guy who owned it was a contractor type who sort of pieced the house together in his spare time. It reminded me of one of those ridiculous looking houses of which I had seen pictures of posted on the internet where someone had tackily added rooms onto a mobile home. The inside was equally disappointing. It was the most unusual home I had ever been in. What décor it had was straight out of the 70's. There was a layer of grime on everything including the wood grain formica countertops, stained wood siding, and the wood grain vinyl floors. When the realtor took me through the home, I laughed in his face. I told him that it was nothing more than a tear down and that I would never stay in that dump. With the money I had recently deposited back into Cahaba Veneer and a little more that the company already had, Cahaba Veneer bought it.

The Affair

When I hired her to work in my office in 2001, Sandy was pregnant with her youngest daughter Abby. Even though I considered her a strikingly attractive woman, there had never been so much as a hint of sexual misconduct between us until my relationship with Audra derailed. Nearly two years older than me, Sandy is about 5' tall, and it is easy to guess that she has a lot of American Indian in her gene pool. It is part of her personality to be quiet and standoffish. In the 1992 Clint Eastwood movie, Unforgiven, Morgan Freeman plays the role of Ned Logan who has an Indian wife. Ned's squaw never said a word but just stared at Munny, played by Eastwood, with reproach during his visit. When Munny comments about how rudely Ned's squaw was treating him, Ned explains that injuns are just that way and that she meant nothing by it. That is Sandy.

When you couple Sandy's good looks with her introverted personality, it is easy to misread her as conceited, when in reality she is just shy and has difficulty interacting with people. Having an employee who is quiet and serious can be a very good thing, and I was pleased to have her working in my office. The more I got to know her, the more impressed I was with her business skills. Unlike others that I have dealt with over the years, she actually listened to my instructions. With an impeccable memory, she rarely forgot anything and hardly ever made a mistake—which caused me to add "perfectionist" to her list of personality traits.

The more I got to know Sandy as an employee, the more impressed I became with her ability to excel in advanced bookkeeping and accounting work. Even still, she would humbly and eagerly do menial jobs. She seemed to sincerely appreciate her job. Her work ethic and attitude starkly contrasted with Audra's. I had grown to view my wife as spoiled, inappreciative, and lazy. Not only was Sandy beautiful, but she was also very humble, smart, and industrious. There was a lot to admire about her and my esteem for her went way beyond the physical. Our conversations gradually became more and more personal and less and less professional. Sandy was not happy at home either, and one thing led to another until it happened.

One afternoon not long after the start of the affair, I was standing in my driveway at home, about to get in my vehicle, when my mother pulled in behind me. She got out to speak and was friendly as usual. It was her habit to pass along various Bible teachings or books that she had acquired from one Christian ministry or another. With a grocery bag hanging from her hand, today would be no exception. I had come to expect hand-me-down material from the likes of Marilyn Hickey, Joyce Meyer, Kenneth Hagin, Kenneth Copeland, Jentzen Franklin, Creflo Dollar, TD Jakes and John/Joel Osteen. After exchanging pleasantries, she explained that she would not stay but that she had come to give me something and would be on her way. Mother looked into my eyes with compassion and embarrassedly said she did not know why this had come up for me but she was sure it was for me. My eyes widened as I thanked her and watched her leave. As soon as she left I pulled out the contents of the bag and to see that it was no hand-me-down.

Still wrapped in plastic, it was an unopened DVD sermon series by Pastor Ed Young entitled "Just Lust." I did not need to listen to the teaching. The title hit me squarely between the eyes.

At first I was irritated with feelings of having my privacy violated. It was totally uncool to have my mother being fed intimate information by God about my indiscretions and it sparked a tinge of rebelliousness. This was further confirmation that my mother's messages from God were 100% legitimate, and that God told her things that she could not know otherwise. Even though I felt like my privacy had been violated, I changed my attitude and decided to embrace God's message as from a loving father who was trying to help me.

I decided I could not continue in this. Only low-down scumbags would cheat on their spouses, and that was not me, even though I had reasons. To be sure, sexual lust had always been a weakness. Since the advent of the internet and porn had become so easy and free, men and women had to be strong to resist such "kryptonite." Sure, I had looked at porn from time to time, but I hated the residual dirty feelings and convictions that always followed. Early in our marriage, Audra caught me looking at it. Seeing the pain and disappointment that it caused made me realize just how dangerous it was. I resolved to cut it off. Somehow, I had gone from a guy who loved my relationship with my wife enough to guard my eyes from porn to someone who would sleep with another woman. I was once the judging Pharisee, quickly condemning anyone who could be so sorry as to do such a thing. The unthinkable had become my reality as I was doing what I had once believed impossible for me.

Something changed inside me the night that I got offended, and I could not quite put my finger on it. The delineation between right and wrong was blurred by arguments that said I deserved to have my needs met by any means even if it meant breaking my marital oaths before God and man. The message delivered by God through my mother was crystal clear. I knew what I was supposed to do, but every time I would make a run from it, I was hooked and would be reeled right back in. I was caught in a cycle of conviction, repentance, weakness, and sin again. Over and over it would happen until Sandy and I both were exhausted from our double-mindedness. I cannot tell you how many times the pendulum swung back and forth. One day it was on and the next day I would tell Sandy it was off. I had become a total basket case and was out of control.

The Deal

Woody's mill had made a fortune selling low grade sweet gum veneers to The Hon Company, who pressed them into curved plywood seats and backs which were covered with foam and fabric and eventually became part of an office chair. Hon would keep Woody's plant busy for about 20 years, but like all big resourceful companies, they were constantly searching for lower cost alternatives. Hon discovered something else to replace veneer and ninety five percent of Woody's orders evaporated. In 2006, with other veneer markets already saturated, Woody's mill was struggling to survive. On the other hand, my mill was humming with the latest improvements and ample flooring orders. Woody was a saver and had no debt, so he could easily retire. His main concern was for his youngest son who needed a job and wanted to be in the veneer business like his father. It was at this time that he approached me to discuss the possibility of a business deal. He and my brother visited my mill and were impressed. My recent financials were stellar and were reviewed by their accountant who helped them form valuations. A meeting with Woody, my mother, brother, and accountants was held and in Birmingham to discuss a possible arrangement. When the meeting was over, we agreed that my brother and I should combine ownership of both veneer mills plus Woody would provide a capital infusion of three million dollars in exchange for a minority stock position for my brother. I would retain control as majority shareholder. Woody had taught me the advantages of holding that position. If the deal went through, for the first time in my career I would be totally debt free!

For me this was a no-brainer. My business had grown to the point that I could use someone with an ownership interest to help me manage operations. Under these terms it made perfect sense to partner with my brother and get out of debt. With my personal life in shambles, at least having some stability at work would be good.

I also had other reasons that I didn't discuss with anyone. With all the money spent on the mill over the last few years, the only way to pay it off was to keep it busy. Just before Christmas of 2006, my main customer called with some frightening news. Contrary to projections, something unexpected was happening in the economy and their orders were much lower than expected. I had a new sense of urgency to get out of debt.

In late January 2007, my marital situation was all the worse, but my dedication to my children continued to prevent me from considering divorce. The house of cards would soon come crashing down when I shared with Audra my plans to partner with my brother. We hardly spoke anymore, but I could not do this deal and keep her completely in the dark. I dared not divulge details but told her in general terms that I was planning to bring my brother in as a minority partner and that I thought it would be wise to do so. As sole owner of the mill, I did not need Audra's consent to complete the transaction, but I did not feel right about moving forward without telling her about it.

Within a day or so of this discussion, she sped to my office with divorce papers in hand. As she confidently served me with them, she explained that the paperwork included a court order restricting me from selling any marital assets to anyone without court approval. After 10 years of marriage, there were no signs of remorse on her face. It was just business and she had just showed me who was boss. Getting it done seemed to take a weight off her shoulders. I was never so humiliated. At the time, I did not understand why she had made such an effort to stop our deal. Months later I learned that she figured that I was preparing to divorce her by reducing the marital estate by selling a large portion of my company to my brother at an undervalued cost. Quite to the contrary, the only thing she stopped was the flow of 3 million dollars into my bank account.

This caught me by surprise, but after further consideration I was glad I did not have 3 million more dollars for her get her hands on. I surmised that she cared more about making a grab for cash than she cared about our marriage and would get her hands on all that she could even if it meant divorcing me to get it. I was relieved that I had not sold before she filed and I was content to let her think she had one upped me because I did not need my company to be worth a lot if I had to pay her half the value. The fight had not just begun, but now the gloves were off.

Deadly Combination

Instantly, I was faced with two of the biggest challenges of my life both personally and professionally. My wife was suing me for divorce and the Great Recession was building steam. I had no idea just how great the recession would become or how long it would take for me to get divorced. I had always known that going through a divorce with Audra would be a bloody war. Her father owned a used truck dealership, and she was no stranger to litigation. Audra's best friend was married to a well-connected attorney who had regularly done work for her father. Back in 1997, when I purchased the mill, I hired Audra's attorney friend to handle the legalities. At this point, he had become a Federal District judge and had tremendous influence within the legal system. As a judge, he could no longer practice law. Nevertheless, there was no doubt in my mind that he was in the background conferring with Audra and her legal team. I felt sure that he would do anything within his power to insure that she was well taken care of.

My first challenge was to hire an attorney. I asked an attorney friend of mine to refer a top of the line divorce guy and he sent me to Cam Parsons. When I met with Cam he said he would represent me, but that he would have to back out if it got too ugly because Audra's dad and his boss did some business together. In an attempt to resolve the matter quickly, he did his best to get a settlement offer from Audra's attorney. When he finally got one it was a ridiculous seven million dollars. After cussing Audra's attorney out, his next call was to me with the news that I needed to find someone else because it was clear that Audra's camp had no intent to quickly resolve this cash cow case. Audra was angry and provoked, and that meant lots of hours could be logged before letting this big fish off the line.

When unscrupulous divorce attorneys land clients with sizeable assets, they will work overtime to prevent resolution until a significant transfer of wealth has taken place to themselves. Such cases are never won by either plaintiff or defendant but rather by the attorneys who profit by such immoral representation practices. One cannot count on a judge to bring order to the situation. Family court judge candidates in Tuscaloosa are selected by the "establishment", who also happen to be the candidate's primary source of campaign funding. The "establishment" is a group of attorneys who make a deal with puppet judicial candidates who, once elected, will help them make money by allowing wealthy client cases to be drug out until the money is gone. All it takes is one side to have unscrupulous representation and then both sides are stuck.

When Cam called to say I was stuck, I called another well-respected attorney named Bill McGuire to ask if he would represent me. He called me back to say that he would love to but could not because Audra had come to see him for a short consultation just before going across town to hire another guy. It was clear that Audra had been working toward putting the screws to me for quite some time, and she had gotten a lot of advice from someone. Bill had a reputation for being one of the best divorce attorneys in town who could get incredible deals for his clients. He believed Audra made an appointment with him for the express purpose of blocking him from representing me. Thankfully, he was angry enough to refer me to Lisa Woods of Birmingham.

Lisa agreed to take my case and also enlisted Steve Wright as co-counsel. Lisa was great in handling the domestic matters while Steve was indispensable when business interests were involved. These two were a legal dream team and I never got the impression that they were trying to string my case along. Pretty soon paperwork was soon flying back and forth. One of the worst parts of dealing with a nasty divorce was the incessant demand for documentation. It seemed that I was bombarded daily with document requests. Audra's lawyers demanded cell phone records, bank statements, financial statements, and the list went on. Even if I sent everything last week, they wanted updated information continuously. No matter what they asked for, my attorneys said I should provide it. They explained that if I refused that they would eventually get it anyway, and that forced extraction would just result in more expensive legal costs. Audra believed that I was hiding money from her, and she was on the hunt. She also had a hunch that I had been cheating on her with Sandy, and she believed that if she could prove it, she would get even more.

When Audra first filed for divorce, I explained to my family that our planned business deal would have to be put on hold until my legal matter with Audra was resolved. They were in no hurry and we continued to operate on the assumption that the transaction would eventually take place. With that in mind, we began to co-mingle assets. I hauled all of Woody's logs to my mill and used them as if they were mine. Anything that could be used by my mill was brought over from Woody's. No money changed hands because when our deal was made it would all be joint property.

In my mind we had a deal, and I would soon be out of debt as soon as I could get divorced. I did not know how much this divorce would cost me, but at least I would soon be able to partner up with my brother and pay off the bank. Business was slowing, but I had no worries because my brother was right there waiting with a big check. Operating on this assumption, I discussed with him an opportunity to improve one of our veneer peeling lines. If we could get it done while we were slow, when the market correction was past we would be ready to put the hammer down. He excitedly agreed, and I put the project in motion. Normally I would have been very cautious about spending capital when business was slowing, but with my brother by my side I had no fear. To accomplish this work would require significant interruptions that were best performed when business was slow. Over the next year, I would spend another five hundred thousand on mill upgrades and as far as I could tell, my judgment had never been better.

After Audra filed for divorce, I had no further thoughts of reconciliation. She had made a public declaration of her hate, and I could not stand to be in the same room with her. I was sure feelings were mutual. I loaded up a few things and moved to the ugly house on the hill in Centreville. I remembered how I said I would never live in that dump 6 months earlier. The dirty little house that I moved into had nothing but patio furniture. The more I looked around, the more concerns I had. No wonder it was so nasty. There was a gap under the front door that a decent-sized mouse could walk right though. After sealing things up as best I could, I tried to clean it, but the grime would not go away. I was repulsed but kept telling myself it was only temporary.

Since the purchase of the property, I had stayed there on occasion. I had a TV, air mattress, and some outdoor furniture indoors, but I stayed only for a day or two at a time. It was not much more than camping out, but she was not there, and there was a lot to be said for that. Proverbs 21:9 says that it is better to live on the corner of a roof than to share a house with a quarrelsome wife and I had come to fully appreciate the wisdom of Solomon. Even though I was miserable, and my love for my wife was practically dead, I was not prepared for divorce or at least I had not been preparing for it like she seemed to have been. Being away from my children left me feeling as though my heart had been ripped out.

I had not investigated the legal aspects of divorce and was flying blind. I did not know that if I left home for a period of time that Audra would be able to claim exclusive use of it, change the locks and tell me where I could go. After all, I bought the house with my money, paid all the bills and my children lived there and that could not be right. Wrong. That is exactly what happened. Ignorance is bliss only until you realize what it has cost you.

The Affair Becomes Public

When Sandy and I started enjoying one another's company, we promised one another that under no circumstances would we ever tell anyone. Period. She was married with two children, I was married with two children, and there was too much hanging in the balance for anyone else to know. We lived in a small community where people thrive on gossip and something like this would make a very big splash in our small pool.

Up until divorce was filed, we never told a soul and had never been caught red-handed but women just know things and Audra had her suspicions. If she did not, she should have. Even though I did not mean it at the moment, there was some truth to what I said that night. Audra knew full well how I was, and it was she who had put me on a crash diet. When Audra filed for divorce, her attorney shared these suspicions with Sandy's husband, a local sheriffs' deputy.

Shortly thereafter, the deputy used his expert interrogation skills on Sandy and elicited a confession. From that point, he put her on lock down. Late that night, when her husband was not looking, she called to let me know. I was in complete and utter dismay. How could she?!! Her husband demanded that she quit her job, and the next day he helped her clean out her desk. All of the sudden, Sandy was gone and unreachable by phone. My entire world had blown up and there were a whole new set of concerns both personally and professionally.

Sandy was indispensable to me as a key member of my office. The remaining staff was in disarray with her abrupt departure and everyone had concerns for their safety. I also wondered if her gun-toting cuckold would retaliate against me personally, or if he would just ask one of his sympathetic buddies to do the job. If I came up missing or dead, I doubted that the local authorities would be very enthusiastic about solving my case. All these concerns were in addition to the impact Sandy's confession would have on my divorce case. I was screwed.

Over the course of the next week, Sandy deliberated as to whether or not she would stay with her husband. Sandy has forbidden me from providing details of her problems with her husband in an attempt to promote healing and avoid hurting her children's relationships with their father. Within a week or so she would decide to leave him and come back to work. I was relieved to have her back both personally and professionally, but it was a Pyrrhic victory. While I continued to remain tightlipped, her confessions had done tremendous damage to our reputations and my divorce case. She also had a divorce to deal with, but when there were few assets to divide, there was not much to discuss.

My brother was a witness to this whole fiasco and was not impressed. He had been patiently waiting for my personal matter to be settled so we could get on with our plans and career together. It had been nearly a year and my personal situation had only gotten worse and there were no signs of an agreement.

Blood was in the water. Armed with knowledge of Sandy's confession, Audra had everything she needed to firmly place blame for our failed marriage on me but primarily on the most despicable of all women—the homewrecker. Audra seemed to have developed a deep hatred of Sandy. She told me that she would be fine with me dating anyone but her. When I objected, I was sure that Hell had no fury like what I saw brewing behind her eyes. I could only imagine how emboldened she had now become. I figured that her lawyers had given her assurance that they would now easily strip and leave me buck-naked on the courthouse steps. Getting half of our marital assets would never satisfy her now.

As far as I knew, Audra refused to accept any role in our failed marriage. I received reports that she was campaigning all over Tuscaloosa as if she were a mudslinging politician. She was very thorough and even called all the members of my family to ask them for support. Sandy's husband threw his hat into the ring as her running mate except his primary voter base was in Bibb County where my business was located. Centreville is a very small town with deep religious roots. Steeped in the Bible belt, there is a church on every corner and down every country road. We would soon see first-hand that there are still plenty of "religious" Pharisees around that are ready and willing to cast the first stone.

Collateral Damage

As far as I was concerned, I did not care if people wanted to speak to me or not. I owned a business in Centreville but did not call it home. I knew how these types were, and I was not about to let any of them dictate to me who I was. On the other hand, Sandy had been living and building her life in that community for nearly a decade, and her children were in the local school system. With her introverted personality, Sandy did not make friends easily. Her ex-husband on the other hand could not keep quiet and was always politicking. After the affair became public, being snubbed by those she thought were her "friends" became a daily event and the emotional toll on her was devastating. While that was tough, nothing would compare to the blindside that was to come. Gossip this juicy would certainly be overheard by the children of those passing the news from household to household. Before long Sandy's oldest daughter was taunted and ridiculed by her peers at school. Her father was relentless with his campaign against Sandy and especially with their own children. Sandy was now faced with the prospect of losing one of her children when her eldest daughter requested permission to stay with her father full-time. This was almost more than she could bear.

My name was being drug through the mud and reputation forever tarnished, but my confidence would not be shaken by what others thought of me, or at least by what most people thought of me. Even though I had blatantly disobeyed clear instructions from

God to turn from lust, I still believed He would see me through this as He had all the other challenges thus far. I believed that God would continue to support me because I had good reasons for my actions and could justify my deviation from the narrow path. My hope was that God would forgive me for this indulgence and let me have my way. I hoped He would not take it personally that I did not want to give it up, and surely he understood that I was only doing what I needed to do.

As far as the business plans with my brother, Sandy's confession changed everything. Amidst all this controversy, my brother and stepfather had become very uncomfortable. The opportunity to join hands with me in a business arrangement was no longer appealing. To gamble such a large investment into a company being run by a person of such immoral character threw up all sorts of red flags. They seemed to believe they could no longer trust me and did not want to be yoked to me should God want to make a correction. My heart was not right with God at this time and to partner with me then would not have been wise. To boot, an economic storm was brewing and the US economy was sputtering. Cash in the bank was looking better and better with each economic update. Shortly after Sandy's confession, my brother and I had a brief meeting during which he asked me if the rumors were true. I told him yes, and he wished me well but told me that he needed to move on. I was not angry with him or Woody. To be honest, I could not blame them for backing out on the deal. Nevertheless, the pull-out was a pronouncement of death over my company.

When business started dropping like a rock at the end of 2006, I went to our main customer in an attempt to secure more business. Not wanting to see any mills close, they were divvying their orders out among several suppliers. That was very considerate of them, but if I did not find a way to get more business soon, I would be the first to go. In exchange for the volume I needed, I agreed to give them significantly better pricing. With the new pricing, I knew that profits would be skinny for a while, but at least I would be able to keep my plant busy and with any luck would be able to pay my bills until business improved. With no debt, I could hunker down and wait out the storm.

My business plans had hope until my brother pulled out. With my debt firmly in place, I had big loan payments that required steady performance and bankers were not impressed with break even. Not only that, I had foolishly spent five hundred thousand more dollars on unnecessary plant upgrades on the assumption that my brother's cash injection would cover that too. Now Woody was demanding that I pay for the assets that had come from his mill. What I thought was going to be an infusion turned into a bloodletting.

During this time, Audra was privy to regular financial statements and from where she stood it appeared that I was cooking the books. To go from record profit levels in 2006 to such modest performance in 2007 was more than she could accept as legitimate. This was just another example of how strangely twisted the whole divorce matter had become. Yes, I had been unfaithful, but

I was not hiding anything else. Audra could not accept the truth. As far as she was concerned, there was not a shred of truth left in me. I tried to have candid conversations to explain the situation with her, but she refused to listen to anything I said. Convinced that her attorney/accountant team would be able to expose my devious attempts to devalue the company, more and more documents were demanded daily and it was wearing me out.

It is one thing to navigate a healthy business through economic storms but quite another to navigate a debt-laden ship through the treacherous waters of severe economic crisis. When the slowdown began, I had never experienced anything like the protracted downturn that was coming over the global economy. The Great Recession was building steam and the housing market bubble was imploding. Most of the wood floors my customers sold were installed in new home construction, and banks would not be making many home loans, and veneer sales would plummet further than ever imagined possible. When I should have been battening down the hatches, there were holes all over my ship that I could not plug. When GM and AIG got their bailouts I was treading water and hanging on for dear life. I spent the cash I did have on legal fees which would average one hundred thousand per year. From 1997 until 2006, I had a line of credit in place but had never drawn on it. I had now come to depend on it to pay my bills.

When 2008 rolled around, my business was performing so poorly that my bank took the oversight of my account away from the local account manager and designated Cahaba Veneer as a "special account." I had not met my loan covenants and the bank had a legal right to foreclose on my business anytime they wanted. Since the bank did not want to own a veneer mill, they offered me a forbearance agreement which meant they would charge me a fee and raise my interest rates to whatever they wanted in exchange for continuing the relationship. This was great news, except my losses would be that much more every month. As the economic crisis took even greater hold, my bank eventually allowed me to pay interest only in an attempt to help me survive.

At the beginning of 2009, the divorce suit was two years old and there were not any signs of progress. So far I had spent over two hundred thousand dollars on legal fees for myself. As far as Audra was concerned, I assumed her father was covering her expenses. Audra's heart had been hardened toward settlement, and the judge refused to try the case. The judge kept telling us to mediate and settle. We went to two court ordered mediations with the same results. With each passing day, I was worth less and less, yet Audra would not accept the facts of my worsening financial situation. Rather than come to grips with things for what they were, she resolved to ride it to the end, even if her gamble meant losing it all. My attorneys were dumbfounded as to how this case could not be brought to an end no matter how great the effort. They told me that in all their experience they had never seen anything like it.

Prodigal Revelation

I had grown accustomed to waking up tired. My ugly little house was supposed to have been a tear-down, but I had been stuck there for years while I continued to make payments on my wife's mansion. Crude as my shack was, it was quiet enough for good sleep, but my mind would not let me rest. Though tempted on occasion to embrace all the negativity, I refused to allow the spirit of depression to take me. I have always believed that where there was a will, there was a way, so I continued to believe things would eventually turn if I remained optimistic. In the past, this method had always worked for me. No matter what happened, I would remain firm in my resolve that God was there for me and that He would help me through whatever challenge I faced. It was true that trusting Him from an early age produced an uncommon confidence and resilience but something was wrong this time.

It used to be that whatever I put my hand to would eventually prosper, but now it seemed that everything I touched resulted in failure. No matter how hard or smart I worked, my situation was only getting worse. I was tempted to believe that there was nothing that could be done. After all, the entire world was in an economic funk and it was all the result of conditions way beyond my control. Watching CNBC discuss big business failures like AIG, Lehman Brothers, and GM made me feel better as I licked my wounds. At least I was not alone and could blame my woes on whole herd of scapegoats. Deep down, I knew better. Death had been steadily creeping up on me over the span of several years. The sin in my life had become the new normal, which made the root of my problems less than obvious. The decline was deceptively slow and steady. I would take one step forward and two steps back. The edge I once had was gone, and the supernatural favor over me had turned into a curse.

Calf-Rope!

September 2009 — I had finally come to my senses. The old hymn says trust and obey for there is no other way, but I was trusting and disobeying. As I crawled out of bed, I decided that I would have to make radical changes before it was too late. I came to realize that my situation closely mirrored that of the Prodigal Son. (Luke 15:11-32) God had not left me. It was I who had chosen to walk away from Him and His protections to follow my own selfish desires. I had squandered my inheritance on loose living. Now that I had spent everything, a severe famine occurred in the country and I began to be impoverished. I worked hard to get myself out of it but I could make no money. As I came to my senses, I remembered how good it had been before I decided to go my own way.

At this point, I realized the degree of my folly. My struggle was not against flesh and blood and not even against the devil and his forces but against God himself. I realized that I had sinned against God and God alone. (Psalm 51:4) I refused to do things His way and decided to go my own way. Even after he went to the trouble of sending my mother to me with the "Just Lust" message, I had ignored his warning. When I refused to obey Him, I found myself contending against my maker. I had been kicking against the goad. It became suddenly clear that all my problems, including my impossible divorce case and business failure, were the result of my disobedience and sin. If God decreed that I would not get divorced, then I would not get divorced. If God decreed that my business would suffer, then it would surely suffer. God has a history of making a point by hardening hearts and refusing to let people go. Even though there was little money left to fight over, could it be that Audra's heart had been hardened and that is why she refused to let me go? I also knew the rest of the prodigal story and that God loves his prodigals. His nature is to leave the ninety nine who are safe to pursue the one lost. Even though I had made a mess of my life and I was a dirty, stinking mess, there was hope. I was desperate to reunite with the faithful God who was patiently waiting for me to start back toward him so he could meet me half way with a gold ring and robe to cover my shame.

> "Make me to hear joy and gladness,
> Let the bones which you have broken rejoice.
> Hide Your face from my sins
> And blot out all my iniquities." Psalm 51:8-9

If you are from the Southeastern U.S., you likely know what "calf-rope" means. If you holler, "calf-rope", it means you realize that you are wrestling with someone who has a hold on you that you cannot get out of. It is what you say when you realize that the strength of your opposition is more than you can bear. It indicates total capitulation. It is to say I give up and you win. It is to tap-out and that is exactly what I wanted to do. I wanted out of that match for good and I never, ever want to be on the wrong side of that fight again. Maybe you are in a situation where you need to holler "Calf-rope!" to God. If you are inspired to do the same, then great—but let me warn you: the relief you seek will not come unless you mean it from your heart, without any reservations.

After nearly three years of divorce war and economic meltdown, I knew there was little time left before it was too late. With a broken and contrite heart, I told God that from then on, I would do whatever He wanted me to do, but in the same breath I demanded that He clearly tell me what that was. I was done playing around. Whatever He wanted me to do, I was going to do it, period. I knew the same God who had broken me could just as easily repair all the damages but I had a lot of questions about what God wanted me to do. I put everything on the table and was very unsure about His will for my life.

I had been holding onto my relationship with Sandy for personal and professional reasons. Through all the personal struggles, what began as lust had developed into very close bonds of love and friendship. We planned to get married if I could ever get divorced, but we no longer dared speculate when that might be. From a professional standpoint, I could not bear the thought of running my business without her. As part of my unconditional reset with God, I knew that my biggest challenge would be putting my closest friend, lover and business partner into his hands.

Sandy and her ex-husband alternated weeks with their daughters. Every other week she would stay with me when she was without kids. I had my girls every other weekend. Whenever either of us had our children with us we would hang out a lot during the day but never stayed together at night. Whenever we were without kids, she lived with me as if we were married. We were pretty much the only friends that either of us had and Sandy was very fragile emotionally and the last thing I wanted was to cause her further pain. That being said, she was in God's hands now and I would do whatever he said. The only problem was that I did not know what he wanted from me so I continued to pray and ask for direction.

From this point forward, I began to journal major events that took place. I decided to show specific dates so that you can see how quickly God responded after I gave my life to Him.

October 4, 2009 — David Morrow, an old friend of mine from Tuscaloosa, called me first thing that Sunday morning. David was relieved when I answered the phone. He said that he had a horrible dream about me and that it was so real that he wondered if it was true. He asked if he could come to Centreville to discuss it. I welcomed his visit. Perhaps God had a message for me which was delivered through this dream.

The morning that David called, I was by myself. Before David's call, I had already asked Sandy if she could come by because I needed to see her. When she arrived, I told her that I had committed my life to God and that I did not know what it meant for our relationship. I tried to comfort her, but she instantly teared up, began sobbing, and without a single word got into her car and left.

I felt horrible and wondered if I had lost her for good.

In the meantime, David called again and said he was coming with his entire family and we agreed to meet at the Twix-N-Tween Restaurant for brunch. I invited Sandy to join us but did not expect her to come. A few minutes after we were seated and very much to my surprise in walked Sandy with a smile on her face. I could not believe it. If she was at all upset, there was no sign. We had a pleasant meal and relocated to my house to continue the visit, but I could not wait to ask Sandy about her remarkable recovery. She told me that she cried all the way home but that when she pulled into her driveway, a feeling came over her that it would be alright and all the hurt and worry instantly left. This was no small miracle and I was amazed. Thank you Lord!

Not long after we got to my house, I pulled David aside and asked him for details about the dream. He said that he had a very restless night and decided to get out of bed to go to the sofa. Once asleep, he experienced an exceptionally vivid vision of a big Mack truck running over and killing me. He described his vision as dark and deadly. As he awoke, he knew it was no ordinary dream when he realized that he had been crying in his sleep and that his eyes were still wet from tears. He said he was upset by my accident, but that the pain and tears came from God's feelings of losing me, and that these feelings had been shared with him. What he saw was so real that he feared for my life and could not wait to get me on the phone to make sure I was still alive. I knew he was acting strangely when I answered the phone, but I had no idea that he thought I might be dead. I needed more, but that was it. Certainly there had to be more. I already knew that I had been walking on thin ice with God, but I had already committed to do whatever he wanted and just needed direction. This dream contained no direction but sounded like a stern warning. When I pushed David for more information he said that the message in the dream was that I had already been told what to do and that I had better hurry up and do it.

Wow! Thanks Dave. I was all the more confused. Was God saying that I needed to completely terminate my relationship with Sandy? Was it his grand design that I be back with my wife?! What did God want? I knew enough about God to know that he was full of surprises so I did not rule anything out.

In order to find the answer I began to back track to the place where I detoured off the path with God. Out of nowhere, it hit me. God never told me to do anything but stop the inappropriate aspects of my relationship with Sandy. That did not include terminating her as an employee. It did not mean that I could no longer be her friend. I knew what he wanted.

I finally knew what I had to, do but this would not be easy. The intimacy that we shared had been one of the few bright sides to the catastrophe that we had both experienced. She was the most attractive woman I had ever known, and we had been together for years. I thought it would have been easier if I never saw her again, but God had no such plans. I got peace that God wanted me to revert to a platonic relationship with Sandy until we could be married but was unsure if I could do it.

October 21, 2009 — I was in the habit of taking my twin daughters on Wednesday night dates. As usual we went out to eat and then to the Barnes and Noble bookstore. They always found something they just had to have, and I would buy them a book or a little something before returning them to their mother. Something very unusual happened that night. I wandered into the Christian section and randomly plucked a book from the shelf titled, *When Pigs Move In* by Don Dickerman. The cover got my attention. It showed a man in a suit except the man's head was that of a pig. The caption below said something about sweeping away demonic influences from my life. It was no doubt weird and creepy. I had never been into anything like that but decided to buy it anyway.

The next morning, I was rushing out the door in an attempt to be at work by our seven o'clock start time and heard a voice in my head say, "I don't need you to run the mill. Stay here and read the book." I knew it was God and that He was talking about the one I bought the previous night so I did as instructed. As I read, I was captivated by the story of Don Dickerman, a Baptist pastor from Texas, and how God called him into the deliverance ministry. His book told amazing stories of people getting free from demonic oppression. I was filled with compassion as my mind wandered to my cousin Suzanna. Again, I heard a voice tell me that He wanted to use me in this ministry but that He would have to clean me up first. As the words were spoken into my mind, it was as if I was standing in the surf of the ocean facing the shoreline, and a wave hit my back knocking me to my knees as the water rushed over and engulfed my entire body. I fell forward onto a foot stool as tears began to flow for what seemed a very long time as my mind raced with memories of failures and my need to repent of heinous sins. My heart was broken as I thought of how I had done so many things that were disgraceful and painful for my heavenly father even though he had done nothing but show his love for me. I begged for His forgiveness with a broken and contrite heart like never before. For the first time in my life I had a sense of God's greater purpose, and my heart burned to be used by Him.

It had been nearly thirteen years since I received the perplexing prophetic message from the Lord through my mother that said, "Pray for the God of Harvest to bring in many souls. You will help minister to them. You are a chosen vessel." I finally got it.

November 2, 2009 — This was a Monday that I will never forget. I had known for several days what I had to do but was dragging my feet. The more I thought about it, the more excuses came to mind. I was thinking things like… *It is too late and there was no reason to stop now…What do you think you will accomplish? You have been with her a long time and everybody knows it…You are just letting Audra control you, and you can't let her keep you from living your life or else she wins…If you could, you would be married to Sandy so in your heart you are already married so God must honor your commitment...God knows you have needs, after* *all he made you...This will be the last straw, when you tell Sandy that you want to stop and want to wait until you can be married, she will leave you for someone who will take care of her needs.*

The unknown aspects of the commitment were torturing me. I had been fighting Audra for 3 years and all indications were that she would hold me in divorce limbo until one of us died. My mind shuddered with thoughts of how long it would be before we could resume the intimacy that I so craved if we decided to wait until we were married. To cut myself off until I could remarry was very hard because the remarry date was unknown and nowhere in sight. It was like going on a fast with no known end date. Nevertheless, nothing else mattered except what God said, and he said stop. I was sure that I had to finally obey Him or else the truck David warned me about would not be rerouted. I took Sandy home for lunch, and instead of going to the kitchen I took her hand and led her to the den. I sat next to her on the sofa and explained that I believed God wanted us to refrain from having sex until we could be married. I was so relieved when she said she believed God was telling her the same thing. I told her that I would need her help and she agreed. We both got down on our knees, repented, and asked God to forgive us of our sins in Jesus' name. We also prayed for Audra and turned her over to the Lord.

This is the part of my story where the real excitement begins. A few days after we repented, I gave Sandy a copy of *When Pigs Move In* and filled her in on how God had come over me while reading it. The following day she began to read it. Later that afternoon she started having some strange numbing sensations in her toes that she never had before. A few days later she told me that she thought the book applied to her. I had the sense that I would handle her problems, but I wanted to finish the Dickerman book so I told her to keep reading her copy, and I would work on finishing mine. Two days later Sandy was in the shower at her home thinking about the strange feelings she had been having so she tried a little self-deliverance according to what she had been reading. Not knowing if there was anything there or not, she started speaking to them. She told them that they did not have permission to be there and to leave in Jesus name. To her surprise she got an answer, and it was a firm, "No!" For the next two weeks Sandy told me that she was having strange sensations such as continued numbness of her toes and one morning she thought she would faint.

November 25, 2009—Sandy and I had gone to Tuscaloosa, bought groceries, and were on the way back to my place. She had not slept well lately and it had gotten dark. As she closed her eyes in an attempt to rest, she immediately tensed up, saying she thought the Dickerman book was making her crazy. She had come to this conclusion because every time she tried to rest she would hear threatening voices. What was happening to Sandy was making me angry, and I told her that the book was making her crazy alright, and that we would take care of what was making her crazy when we got to my house.

Sandy has never had an ounce of fat on her since I have known her. Devoid of all insulation, she is very cold natured. It was below freezing that night. When we got to my house, I was focused on dealing with her spiritual problems, but before getting started we were in and out unloading groceries. Even though my mind was distracted by the upcoming ministry, she got my attention when she said she was hot. Her cheeks were flushed while my teeth were chattering. As cold as I was, I knew some unusual things were going on inside her one hundred pound body. She energetically helped me put up the groceries and announced that she was going to get a shower and be off to bed. I looked at her and smiled because I knew who was controlling her at that moment. I told her and them: Not so fast. Come on back here and let's do this.

If these demons thought that they would run roughshod over my woman any longer then they had another thing coming. I did not feel entirely prepared but the situation was urgent because they were making Sandy feel as though she was going crazy. Her demons had lost their cover and were no longer content to lurk behind the scenes as sneaky manipulators. They were disturbed and were becoming bolder by the minute. As strange as all this was, I was remarkably at ease considering I was about to go head to head with demons. Stranger still, from this day forward there has been an eagerness inside me to destroy the kingdom of darkness and relish every opportunity to be used by God to set others free.

Disparaging Deliverance

I understand full well that talk about deliverance is just plain weird and will freak many people out. At best, I am sure that many who read this book will find talk about demons and deliverance to be disconcerting. I also think it is safe to assume that many readers who are made uncomfortable by the direction of my story consider themselves to be Christians. Early on, I also had feelings of discouragement relative to the unusual nature of my calling, but I had to repent of those thoughts. The fact is that a huge percentage of Jesus' recorded ministry are accounts of Jesus casting demons from people. Much of the Word of God speaks of the mission of Jesus in terms of deliverance and that He came to set captives free. It was blaringly obvious that God's call on my life was consistent with the sacred texts but that it was my culture that took issue with my calling. Who was I to complain that my Lord and Savior would call me into a ministry that was clearly one very close to His own heart? Jesus did not retain the ministry of deliverance and healing to himself but rather equipped his followers and sent them out to do the same. Who was I to disparage His call to serve just as He called the twelve disciples in Mark 6:7, "And he called unto him the twelve, and began to send them forth by two and two; and gave them power over unclean spirits;" Jesus' commission extended way beyond the twelve as seen in Luke 10:1,17,18,19, "After these things the Lord appointed other seventy also, and sent them two and two before his face into every city and place, whither he himself would come… And the seventy returned again with joy, saying, Lord, even the devils are subject unto us through thy name. And he said unto them, I beheld Satan as lightning fall from heaven. Behold, I give unto you power to tread on serpents and scorpions, and over all the power of the enemy: and nothing shall by any means hurt you."

I determined in my heart that I would not let my identity be dictated by what other people thought but by the Word of God. Some might say that deliverance is just too strange, weird, and unnatural. I agree, when God gets involved, many unexplainable and supernatural things can be expected. If God wanted to honor me with a calling to see miracles in Jesus' name as he healed and set people free, then I would not let anyone rob me of that privilege.

Before I tell you about Sandy's deliverance experience, I need to give you some background information about what I learned from *When Pigs Move In* by Don Dickerman. There was a lot of new information for me in this book, and even though I knew God placed it in my hand and told me to read it, some of it was so fantastic that I had reservations. My personal experiences would eventually remove all doubt.

Dickerman teaches that for demons to present, they have had or do have permission from God to be there. In the majority of cases, it is the person's sin that triggers permission. If the person with the demon has sincerely made Jesus their Lord, then they qualify for freedom, but demons do not necessarily leave immediately at conversion. As new believers submit themselves to God in ever increasing levels of sanctification, new levels of freedom will be achieved. The reverse also is possible. Christians can embrace sin at any time that could result in future demonic permissions.

To remove a demon is not complicated, but attempts to remove them when their permission remains intact will fail miserably. The key to being free is to be fully submitted to the Lord and to honestly seek to line your will up with God's will. The presence of a demon indicates an area of our lives that we have not submitted to God. When we sincerely submit that sinful area to the Lord, repent of it, and claim freedom in Jesus' name, the demonic powers which are there to promote sin in that area have lost their rights. Once legal permission is cancelled and authority is properly exercised over them, they will have no other choice but to leave in the name of Jesus. Please note that demons are legalists. Even though their host has made Jesus their Lord and repented of the sin that gave them lease to occupy, they will often remain until served an eviction notice and commanded to leave in the name of Jesus.

Consistent with the Bible, demons have personal names like we do and specific departments and job titles. For example my name is Pete and I work in wood processing as an owner/operator. A demon might have a name such as Drake, he works in the Lust department and his job to promote porn in the person that he occupies. Demons are organized hierarchically such that each department may have many workers who report to a common department leader. These department head demons prefer to be called "princes" and the departments that they manage as their "kingdoms." This is important for the deliverance minister because we want to deal with the princes only. Once the prince demon had been properly dealt with, he and his entire kingdom of worker demons can be ejected at one time. Dealing with peon demons one at the time is inefficient and very time consuming.

Sandy's Freedom

I had a four-seater high top table with stools in the den behind the sofa, and it was there that I asked Sandy to sit opposite me with my back against the wall. I had my Bible, Dickerman book, and pen and paper. I started with a short prayer asking for God's help and then followed the outline in the Dickerman book. I led her through prayers of renunciation, breaking of soul ties, repentance, confessions of being born again, Jesus as Savior, Lord, deliverer, healer and that He has broken the power of the curse. Importantly, I did not forget to command all of her demons to be bound in the name of Jesus.

It is hard to describe the feelings I had at this point. As I commanded a prince demon to identify himself either by name or function, I was suddenly overwhelmed by the feeling that this was all ridiculous nonsense. Such thoughts quickly vanished when without delay a demon took over and spoke through Sandy's mouth. There were none of the theatrics common to Hollywood horror flicks but in a tone of voice that I had never heard from Sandy's mouth before, the demon said his name was Michael. I asked him if he was a prince demon, and he said yes. I asked what his function was, and he said that he was there to promote sexual sin. I asked him if he had rights to be there, and he said *yes*. I demanded to know what Sandy had done that gave him the right, and he responded *unforgiveness*. At my request, the demon identified exactly the person Sandy needed to forgive.

At that point, I needed to counsel Sandy to forgive this person and remove the demon's rights so that I could command him to leave. When I called her name, immediately the demon left, and Sandy was back. It was as if she had been asleep the entire time I spoke to the demon. She remembered none of the conversation with him whatsoever. I filled her in, and told her she would need to forgive the person named by the demon. I led her through confessions of having forgiven this person followed by asking God to now forgive her and set her free.

When I addressed him by name, Michael was immediately back, and Sandy was gone. I asked him again if he had still had permission, and he said *no*. Satisfied that I had what I needed, I told him to gather all his junior demons together, clean up all the damage they had done in this temple of the Holy Spirit, heal, restore, and repair everything to exactly the way that Jehovah God intended her to be, recall any of himself that he had passed down to her children, and after doing so, come out of her and go directly into the pit right now in Jesus' name. Sandy slumped over the table with her arms stretched forward and began to cough. I sat in silent amazement as I watched the physical effects on her body as the process unfolded. After a few minutes she had fully recovered. I asked her how she felt, and she said she felt good so we decided to move on.

Over the next hour, I came face to face with four more demonic "princes" with different "kingdom" agendas. One was there to promote feelings of unworthiness; another to attack her faith in

God, herself and others; another said he was the "boss" and finally the last one said his kingdom was death and that he was there to promote depression and suicide. Each of these demon princes had their rights to be there because of unforgiveness of various people and when she forgave them, God set her free. As I went from one prince to the next, destroying and removing their kingdoms, I thought to myself that this was too easy—but they had some tricks up their sleeves. When I commanded one of the prince demons to identify himself, Sandy looked up and began pointing at something behind me and above my head. There was only about five feet between me and the wall, so if there was something there, it was close. A look of utter horror was on her face. She shouted my name as if the thing she saw was about to get me. The hair stood up on the back of my neck, and I refused to look. Sandy then hopped off the stool and ran sideways in terror away from the table never taking her eyes off what she saw behind me. She ran right into a support column which ended the theatrics. I was binding them again in the name of Jesus and told them that was enough and that there would be no more of that. Sandy returned and we finished without further incident. She remembered none of it.

Before we got up from the table, it came over me to tell her that God always wins. She was stunned. She explained that the threat that she heard earlier on the way home was that she would not win. Thankfully, God had the last word.

I was overjoyed with the success of giving those demons a beat down but more importantly that Sandy was free of them. She said that she felt lighter, as if a weight had been lifted from her shoulders. We played an Avalon album as we skipped and danced all over the house, praising God for what he had done. When the celebration was over, I hopped in the shower. When I got out the first thing I heard was a spoon clanging against a bowl, and when I saw her eating ice cream, I could hardly believe it. Lactose intolerant was an understatement in describing the sensitivity of her digestive system to milk or dairy products. I learned from experience to never go anywhere without Lactaid. I chastised her, and she just smiled and smirked. She said it had come over her that she was healed. I remembered that demons cause sickness and disease and many were now gone. That is why I was taught to command them to heal, restore, and repair everything before leaving. Duh, I should have been expecting it. For the first time in her life, she enjoyed a bowl of ice cream without a stomach ache.

I was nothing more than a prodigal who God delivered and put to work delivering others—a prodigal deliverer. Unusual as it was, God had given me purpose, and it thrilled me to have a new lease on life.

This changed everything. All of the sudden, I had a new found appreciation for how real God was, the truth of His Word, and how dangerous it was to deviate from it. God had just shown me "marvelous things", and the thirteen year old birthday prophesy continued to unfold.

I could not wait to tell my mother the news, but when I got her on the phone, of course she already knew. As a matter of fact, she had received another message from God and was waiting for an opportunity to give it to me. A few days later I met mother, and she gave me the new message written in her hand. When I saw the date at the top, my jaw dropped. She received the message the day after the last day that Sandy and I had sex.

October 30, 09

It is well, it is well with my soul.

Pete is hissed for.—God has gathered him. God has redeemed him from all unrighteousness. Pete is serving God in a mighty way, reaching out to people in need of deliverance. Pete is a mighty man of God reaching out to be fishers of men and not money. Money will come, but it will be second place. Having put lust under his feet to fulfill his calling in life. His new love for his fellowman outpours in his very existence. Every thought is aimed toward serving mankind. He will establish kingdoms of grace and love and be a beacon of hope. He will pursue an appetite of love over lust, causing many to be set free. The world will have no pull on him because worldly desires have no power on him, only a desire to do God's will. Gossip is far from him. He stays away from negative forces. His lips only speak good and encouraging words that edify. His feet walk the straight and narrow path that leads to faithfulness in God's plan. His strength of character is unshakable. He listens to the voice of almighty God and does his pleasure. He is a tall tree unshakable and immovable. His voice will be pleasant to the ear with plenty of wisdom. He will be secure in the Lord, getting his strength from His Word. Prayer will be his second nature, abounding in wisdom and insight. Praises will flow freely from his mouth. Songs of praise will be his second nature. Speaking in tongues and interpretation will be his gifts. Silence and meditation are his strong points, ceasing the enemy. Books will be written, testimonies will be given, people will be helped, set free and delivered. The power of God will flow throughout his life and people will be healed. He will experience the love of God like never before, cleansing him from all unrighteousness. Staying straight because the fear of God is all over him, consuming him like a fire. Ungodly thoughts will be cast down, never to consume him again. Lust is a thing of the past. Godliness is first place.

Alleluia, thank you Jesus, Praise the Lord.

Yet again, my mind was blown. There was simply no other way that my mother could have known about my calling into the deliverance ministry except that God told her. It was a total blindside for me until I bought the Dickerman book. By the time I got the newest message, some of it had already come to pass, but even more exciting were the things yet to unfold. One of them is coming to pass right now as I write this book.

Birthday letter from God, through my mother, 1996

Pete - Nov. 19, 1996

For your Birthday: God has a special message for you. He loves you very much. When you were very young I chose you as my very own. Now that you are grown and have many responsibilities you are much of my concern. Don't ever dispair and think that I'm not there. I'm always here for you. I rejoice in your thankfulness. I have great pleasure in your needing me. I stand by your side in all your needs. I love you very much my son. Rejoice and give thanks for about what I am doing in your life. Praise Father, Son and Holy Ghost. Let your light shine. Forgiveness is a fruit I want to give to you. This fruit makes everything sweet in your life. When you give

it away - it sets you free. Praise
Father, Son and Holy Ghost. Whisper
into my ear your every fear. I will
wipe them away. Shine like I want
you to with the brightness of my
love. Never be a people pleaser. Only
try to please me. I'm really the
only one that counts. Your will
should be changed to my will. I
desire to bless you. I desire to
make you an overcomer. I
desire your love. I desire your
respect. I need you and want
you as my own. Pray for the
God of harvest to bring in many
souls. You will help minister unto
them. You are a chosen vessel. Rise
high, soar high over the problems of life.
Always give them to me and I will take
care of them. You are a Priesthood, a
royal nation, I plan to show you great
and marvelous things. So be it —

Letter from God, through my mother, Oct. 30, 2009

Oct. 30th '09

It is well, it is well with my soul.

Pete is hissed for. - God has gathered him. God has redeemed him from all unrighteousness. Pete is serving God in a mighty way, reaching out to people in need of deliverance. Pete is a mighty man of God reaching out to be fishers of men and not money. Money will come, but it will be second place. Having put lust under his feet to fulfill his calling in this life. His new love for his fellowman outpours in his very existence. Every thought is aimed toward serving mankind. He will establish Kingdoms of grace and love and be a beacon of hope. He will persue an appetite of love over lust, causing many to be setfree. The world will have no pull on him, because worldly desires have no power on him, only a desire to do God's will. Gossip is far from him. he stays away from Negative forces. His lips only speak good and encouraging words that edify. His feet walk the straight and narrow path that leads to faithfulness in God's plan. His strength of character is unshakable. He listens to the voice of almighty God and does his pleasure. He

Mallie

is a tall tree unshakable and immovable. His voice will be pleasant to the ear with plenty of wisdom. He will be secure in the Lord, getting his strength from his word. Prayer will be his second nature, abounding in wisdom and insight. Praises will flow freely from is mouth. Songs of praise will be his second nature. Speaking in tongues and interpretation will be his gifts. Silence and meditation are his strong points, ceasing the enemy. Books will be written, testimonies will be given, people will be helped, set free, and delivered. The power of God will flow throughout his life and people will be healed. He will experience the love of God like never before, cleansing him from all unrighteousness. Staying straight because the fear of God is all over him, consuming him like a fire. Ungodly thoughts will be cast down, never to consume him again. Lust is a thing of the past. Godliness is first place. Alleluia, thank you Jesus, Praise the Lord.

My house prior to my disobedience

My humble dwelling; After I chose to ignore God's messages

My Deliverance

As I sorted out all the events of late, a major realignment took place. Instead of viewing myself as a businessman, I was coming to view myself as a minister of God who peeled veneers on the side. My business became no more than a means of support for my new found purpose in life. Making an impact for God in the lives of others for all eternity easily trumped my desire to make money and be a successful businessman.

Instead of believing that the Bible was true, I had now experienced the truth and power of God's Word and craved more. I began to read and study the Bible like never before. I would find myself pondering scriptures and talking to God constantly about them. I was purifying my mind with such fervor that all unnecessary distractions were ignored. I rarely watched TV or even the news. I had no desire to do anything other than study the Bible, and listen to praise and worship music, and preach to my congregation of one—Sandy. All other music left me feeling empty, so I erased the secular music on my iPod and started buying loads of praise and worship music that I played constantly at home and in my car. It was not like I was fasting from secular music. I just did not like it anymore. I could not handle most of the lyrics and to listen to anything other than praise and worship music seemed like a waste of time.

At the time I did not realize it, but I was fasting from what had a hold on me. I had been over six weeks without sex and was replacing it with something much better. One night I was all alone lying in bed, listening to worship music and praying. Suddenly it was like blinders were removed from my eyes and I could see clearly what the spirit of sexual lust looked like. A beautiful façade melted away to reveal a truths of unspeakable horror and filth. My heart was deeply grieved by the thought of having embraced something so nasty, ruthless and evil. Sincerely repulsed, for the first time in my life, I hated it. Rolling over onto my stomach, I buried my face into my pillow and wept while asking God to forgive me. Just then, I felt something on my back. Wearing nothing but boxer shorts, it felt like a large spider was moving around between my shoulder blades. I hate spiders worse than anything. I leapt out of bed turning on lights and trying to shake it off. I was totally freaked and turned my bed upside down, looking for whatever it was, but found nothing. After thinking more about it, I am convinced the spirit of lust left me that night.

Most believers accept the existence of angels and demons, but the Bible holds only vague clues as to the extent of their interactions with humans. I have learned that our dealings with them are much more common and continuous that I ever believed. My experiences with Sandy proved to me just how easy it was to allow a spiritual enemy to gain access and some level of control. All it took was for her to be offended. For each instance of unforgiveness, there was a corresponding demonic entity. If that is all it takes, who among us is not susceptible? I do not think that possession is the proper term to describe most situations. It is more accurate to describe Christians as being oppressed rather than possessed. I believe it is very likely that most of us either have or have had direct demonic influence during the course of our lives. Any way that you prefer to look at it, demons are against us, and to give them permission to enter into our bodies just gives them a higher level of access to do the same things they have been doing since we were born. Consider the following scripture in light of this discussion. John 2:24-25 says, "But Jesus did not commit himself unto them, because he knew all men, and needed not that any should testify of man: for he knew what was in man."

This world is full of marvelous things that I cannot see that I believe exist. For example, I cannot see radio waves, yet I tune into radio stations. I cannot see electricity move along the wires that feed my house, yet it is easy to tell when it is not there. There are many things that we as humans have learned to believe in that we can sense only through external equipment and technology so it should not be such a stretch to believe there are a few more still hidden from us. I had now witnessed the spirit realm and come to understand just how closely spirit beings interact with every one of us.

Beware of Demonic Schemes

If you get anything from my book, please get this: If you are a human, you are under the attack of the enemy. Demons are particularly interested in occupying the bodies of people, especially Christians, so they can trash what God has put in order. There are things that you, as a Christian, can do that result in permissions for them to gain a higher level of access to you. Period. In the parable of the Unforgiving Debtor in Matthew 18, Jesus teaches that those of us who come to him for forgiveness of our sins and yet refuse to forgive others of their sins will be turned over to the tormentors. Tormentors are demons. We must obey God's command to love and forgive one another unconditionally. Failure to forgive opens the door to the enemy to come in and defile us who are called to be clean temples of the Holy Spirit. Please do not be a victim of ignorance or refusal to believe this biblical truth as I was.

I now understand in depth what happened the night that I got offended by Audra. I opened the door for the enemy to come in, and the war began. What began as a mole hill turned into a mountain that destroyed my marriage and caused untold pain and devastation, which I am still recovering from today. It all started with one offense that led to another and another that resulted in more and more demonic activity until it was a full blown train wreck. The enemy does not come except to kill, steal, and destroy. Forgive everyone who has ever hurt you, including yourself. God says you are worthy. Adopt a spirit of unconditional love and forgiveness toward everyone, regardless of how they treat you, for you have no pride or ego to defend as a humble follower of our foot washing example named Jesus. Offenses must come, but ask God to show them to you and help you release them to Him. Do it and continue to do it daily as new offenses come. Jesus tells us plainly how important forgiveness is in Matthew 6:14-15, "For if ye forgive men their trespasses, your heavenly Father will also forgive you: But if ye forgive not men their trespasses, neither will your Father forgive your trespasses." I know this is a controversial statement, but I believe that a Christian's salvation depends on our forgiveness and continued forgiveness of all others. How will we make it to heaven if God has not forgiven us? As we show mercy to others, we triumph over judgement. We have this opportunity only because of what Jesus did for us on the cross. Consider the following verse in light of this discussion, "And he said to them all, 'If any man will come after me, let him deny himself, and take up his cross daily, and follow me.'" Luke 9:23. Whatever offenses we receive throughout the course of our day, we must come to a place of giving them to God. We must obey the command of Jesus to love one another unconditionally by sacrificing our pride and ego daily. We must resolve to adopt a spirit of forgiveness such that we pattern ourselves to the loving savior who died for us.

Suzanna

Following the success with Sandy, I could not get my cousin Suzanna off my mind. From the time that I met her demons in the beach condo, I wished that I could help her but, until now, I had no clue about what to do. There are thousands of Christian churches in Alabama, but few of them would allow you to discuss helping someone get rid of demons in church much less offer to help you do it. My heart burned to reach out to Suzanna. I prayed for God to give me the chance to minister to her because I thought she might be hard to reach. After a few days, I got her phone number from a relative. She answered my first call and readily accepted my offer to meet. She was still living in Gulf Shores, and I doubted she would drive four hours for our meeting, so I offered to meet her there.

The plan was to drive down on Friday, spend the night, and meet with Suzanna during the day on Saturday. I asked Sandy if she would go with me, but knowing the agenda she was less than enthusiastic. Judging from her firm stance, I resolved to go it alone, but at the last minute I was surprised when she said she would go and that she felt like God wanted her to.

December 19, 2009 — A family member agreed to let us stay in her beach house for the weekend and meet with Suzanna there. Sandy and I awoke in Gulf Shores Saturday morning. I had not slept well—in a good kind of way, like a kid on Christmas Eve. We were expecting Suzanna to arrive sometime around noon so we got going early with a caffeine and calorie fix from Waffle House. Gulf Shores was pleasantly quiet that time of year, and the abandoned beach house was the perfect venue for our meeting. The last time I saw Suzanna at our grandmother's condo she had just gotten married. At this point she had a two year old daughter.

It did not come as a surprise that our agreed upon meeting time came, and Suzanna was a no-show. As the sun marched across the sky, I grew increasingly anxious and irritated, but I knew there were evil powers working overtime to prevent the meeting.

An interesting aspect of the deliverance ministry is that it is difficult to make an appointment with someone to help them get rid of their demons without their demons knowing about it. We know from scripture that they will do anything they can to avoid removal. I have had many people tell me of strange things that happened leading up to their appointment that were obvious efforts to prevent it from taking place. I learned it was a good idea to pray for people as much and as early as possible leading up to the appointment. It is also a good idea to start binding the demons in the person in the name of Jesus well in advance of the meeting. Prayer is key to getting this done, but nothing is more important than the resolve of the person to be free and she was ready for some relief from anywhere she could find it.

It was nearly dark before she arrived with her daughter in tow, apologizing and saying that she had difficulty finding the house. Suzanna was disheveled and jittery. She had been to this house many times for family gatherings but had somehow gotten lost. I was not expecting her to come with her child and I wondered if that was the reason Sandy had received her last minute commissioning to attend. Suzanna had appeased her daughter with a large chocolate bar which was now all over her face, hands, and clothes. Immediately Sandy began to help by offering to clean up the little girl.

After quieting her daughter by laying down with her for a few minutes in one of the bedrooms, Suzanna came back to us and said she was ready. The three of us sat at a wrought iron glass topped dining table in the living room. Sandy was at the head, while Suzanna and I sat on either side of her facing one another.

I explained a little bit of the deliverance process to Suzanna and went straight to work. After learning what I had about Sandy's demons being there because of unforgiveness, I pressed into the subject with Suzanna. I told her that she would have to be willing to forgive everyone who had offended her, for any reason, or else God would not forgive her and set her free (Matt.6:14-15). After she repeated after me all the standard confessions and renunciations, I bound all the evil spirits in or around her in Jesus name and started with the commands.

Immediately after commanding a prince demon to identify himself, Suzanna's countenance and voice changed to something very sinister and irritated. Sandy was far from comfortable, but I had encouraged her to be my sidekick prayer partner. When I started messing with the demons, she looked as though she wanted to get the heck out of dodge. I was proud of her because she hung in there with me praying under her breath. When the demon assumed control of Suzanna's faculties, Sandy seemed to want to look away as if to avoid the demon's attention yet was watching in the corner of her eyes as she continued to pray. She would later tell me that it was scary and fascinating at the same time and that she would have never believed it if she had not seen it. As I was preparing to address the demon, who had identified himself as a prince demon of "death," the demon took the opportunity to threaten me and my family. I had not yet opened my mouth but was about to respond that I did not care what he said when he mocked me in a deeply sarcastic tone, "I don't care!" I laughed and thanked the demon for clearing that up. I had always wondered if thoughts were open communication for spirit beings. The Bible clearly says that God knows our thoughts, but what about other spiritual creatures such as angels, demons and the devil? The demon knew my response before I said it, and as far as I was concerned that settled it. It was no wonder they knew exactly the areas in which to most effectively tempt us.

Angered by my response the demon pounded Suzanna's fists onto the glass table and made such a clamor that the child awoke and began to cry. Sandy was pleased to attend to the girl in a separate room so Suzanna and I could continue. I bound them again in the name of Jesus and ordered that there would be no more such shenanigans. After four hours of intense ministry, ten demonic kingdoms were torn down and removed in Jesus name. With each removal she reportedly felt better and lighter, as more and more weight was lifted from her shoulders. One of the prince demons said he ran a kingdom of "addiction." When this one was told to leave with all his minions Suzanna said she could see little black things about the size of silver dollars leave her mouth and run along the floor and scatter away from her. When I was satisfied that all had been done that could be, we called it a night and Suzanna left with her child after a brief post deliverance celebration where we praised God for this victory.

While it was late, and I had slept little over the last few days, I was so fired up that I hardly noticed and slept little again that night as my mind churned with all the truly marvelous things that God had shown me. Was this for real? Was I really taking authority over angels who had fallen with the devil from heaven? Who was I that God would reveal such mysteries of the spirit realm to me and enable me to serve in this capacity? I was honored and humbled.

Spirit of Cancer

December 20, 2009 — The next day, Sandy and I drove back to Centreville. I would not rest much that night either because I had invited several of my friends who used to go to church with me in Tuscaloosa at Calvary Baptist to come down and cook out. I could not wait to tell them about all the things that were going on of late. Several of the guys were in the Sunday school class the day that I shared about Suzanna busting into grandma's condo so they were all ears to hear more of the story. These men had known me for a long time and knew me well enough to know that I was not making this stuff up. Sandy helped me cook. While we were eating, I was doing much of the talking, but when she shared her testimony, it was so quiet that you could hear a pin drop. After eating, she left, and we had great fellowship.

The next day was Monday and I went to work as normal, but by the end of the day my weekend of all-nighters had caught up with me. Sandy's children were with her ex-husband so she would be staying at my place and hopefully cooking more that week. I showered before supper and after eating it took all my strength to brush my teeth, pull the covers back, and crawl into bed at seven o'clock.

The second I put my head on my pillow, I quickly began to fade into deep sleep, but during the transition something very strange happened. My mouth began to move involuntarily as someone else said, "In the name of Jesus, spirit of cancer come out of her."

Stranger still, when the speaker got to "cancer", I felt physical resistance on my jaws like rubber bands that were trying to keep my jaws closed and keep me from saying the word. Even though "cancer" was reduced to a slur, it registered in my mind loud and clear as I fell into a deep sleep.

At around three in the morning, I awoke refreshed after eight hours of solid sleep. I did not know Sandy had come to bed, but all the lights were out, and she was sound asleep next to me. As I gathered my bearings, I remembered the strange thing that happened as I was dozing off to sleep, and I pondered on it. Spirit of cancer come out of her, hmm…my mind went to Sandy and the fact that she was scheduled for a full hysterectomy in January. Her gynecologist, Dr. Samuel Gray of Birmingham advised that she have the procedure after her last routine exam indicated the presence of pre-cancerous cells. When Sandy told me about it I gave it little thought because she had minimized it as a precautionary measure.

As I laid there, quietly having these thoughts, Sandy suddenly flung all the covers off her upper body. I rolled over to my side and watched her in amazement. For some reason her body temperature had risen, and I could see tiny beads of sweat glistening on her forehead from the light emitting from the alarm clock numbers. It was three o'clock in the morning, three days from Christmas, and this skinny woman was sweating in bed which seemed to coincide with me thinking about, "In the name of Jesus, spirit of cancer come out of her."

I got the message. I did not think that Sandy was awake, but I leaned in close to her ear and whispered that I was about to pray for her. She did not respond so I placed my hand on her belly and repeated exactly what I heard the night before, "In the name of Jesus, spirit of cancer come out of her." I said it over and over with increasing emphasis. I stopped after about the fourth time when her back arched sitting halfway up before she laid back down. I asked her if she was ok. She asked what just happened and I filled her in. She said she felt good except that her eyes were burning a little. I explained to her that I believed she was healed and would not need to have the hysterectomy. I was then given instructions for her. She was supposed to schedule an appointment with Dr. Gray for a re-check. Everyone having to do with her visit was to be told of why she wanted to be reevaluated. This included the person that took the appointment by phone, staff at the front desk, nurses and doctor. They were to be told that she was there because she believed that God had healed her. Not a bad deal in exchange for getting healed and not having to go through surgery. This request certainly has plenty of precedent where Jesus orders those who have been healed to go and show themselves and give testimony for what He has done.

Miracles of Fasting

December 30, 2009 — I began my first ever food fast. Four days earlier I bought Jentzen Franklin's book, *Fasting*, and was inspired. The copycat that she was, Sandy read it too and started a week long fast on January 1, 2010.

January 2, 2010 — This day would prove to be one of the most special days of my life. My mother called me and said that my sister was in need of ministry. I had given copies of the Dickerman book to various family members for Christmas. My sister had been reading her copy and began to exercise her rights as a believer to take authority over her spiritual enemies. When she did so, she started having problems. Demons prefer to accomplish most of their work behind the scenes surreptitiously. This policy changes if their homestead is threatened. When disturbed, they will take more obvious steps to protect themselves that often exposes their presence.

My sister had no clue that she had demonic issues, but her recent educational activities brought them to the surface. She started having nightmares and other nighttime disturbances. Her case was very much different than that of Suzanna. There were very few indications that an enemy was in the camp. Her heart for the Lord was sincere, yet something was not quite right. She was always in church, leader of a Sunday school class, listening to Christian music, in women's small groups and Bible studies, and strictly enforced respect for God in her household. So, when my mother told me she needed help from me, the black sheep of the family, I was intrigued. I had to laugh as I realized God's sense of humor in all this. Here I was with my reputation totally trashed but in a recently reconciled, intimate relationship with God called to minister to someone whose reputation was flawless yet in need of freedom.

I almost missed the biggest blessing of my life. My mother called on Friday and asked if I would make myself available for my sister on Saturday, but she did not know any details. I was expecting a call from my sister early on Saturday to tell me what time she wanted to meet, but she never called. I did not have much else to do, but I felt like I had been disrespected and treated like my time did not matter. As the sun was going down, I hopped onto my bike for a little exercise and to blow off some steam. My heart rate increased from more than the exercise. As I propelled my bike along, anger and pride rose up inside me as I imagined my sister loathing the idea of humbling herself to receive ministry from such as me. By the time I got back to my house, the temperature outside was dropping like a rock and Sandy had a fire roaring in the fireplace with her feet propped up watching TV. I had resolved that I would not go that night. Just as I was about to warm myself by the fire, my phone rang and it was my mother asking if I would meet that evening. To begin with, I said it was too late and that I should have been called earlier. My mother was very gracious and said she understood but that my sister could not meet any other time in the near future. Just before saying goodbye

I caught myself, reversed my answer, and said I would do it.

When I arrived, I was surprised by the number of people at the house. Both of my sisters were there with their families with kids running around everywhere, and my mother was there too. After awkwardly visiting for a few minutes with everyone, I withdrew to the basement with my sister and her husband to get started.

The uneasy couple sat together on a sofa and I sat in a chair on the end closest to my sister. I discussed possible causes of demonic problems. We covered unrepented of sin, generational sin, and, in particular, the sin of unforgiveness. I asked her if she knew of anything she needed to repent of and she said she did not. I pressed her on the subject of unforgiveness and she acted as if she had thought about it and that there was nothing there. I then led her in the standard prayers of confession and repentance followed by commands that a prince demon to identify himself. Nothing happened. There were no indications that she had any issues and it seemed like she was good. I was at a loss and this was new ground for me. Maybe nothing was there. Just before giving up, it came over me to pray and ask the Holy Spirit for his opinion on the matter. I turned the floor over to him and asked Him to reveal to my sister if there were any issues He knew of. After a brief pause, she suddenly leaned forward and put her face into her hands with her elbows on her knees. I did not know what was going on, but it appeared that her eyes were closed and that she was praying. She began sniffling, and I saw tears running off her face. I exchanged glances with my brother-in-law as he moved closer and put his arm around her. I got up for some tissues and when I returned the situation had gotten all the more intense. I offered her the tissues and interrupted to ask what was going on. She told me to leave her alone because God was talking to her.

I was watching and listening to this remarkable scene as God completely took over and did the heavy lifting. After a few minutes I picked up on a pattern. I could not hear what God was saying to her, but I could hear what she said to Him. She would say, "Yes Lord, I am only your servant. Yes Lord, I release him/her to you." Then a pause and she would say it again, "Yes Lord, I am only your servant. Yes Lord, I release him/her to you." After watching this for a little while, I had the sense that I should give her some privacy so I went upstairs to give mother a report. Twenty or so minutes later I went back down to see that God was finished, and the look on her face indicated she had been through the ringer. I asked her what happened and she said that God was writing the names of people on a chalkboard in her mind and was demanding that she forgive them one by one. When she agreed, he erased it and wrote another name until she had forgiven everyone who had ever offended her. She said the list went all the way back to middle school and included the names of people she had not seen or thought of in many years. She had completely forgotten about many of the offenses and the people yet God had impeccable records of every person who had ever offended her in any way that she had not forgiven. Over and over God showed her the name, told her she was only His servant, and demanded that she forgive them. This went on for about thirty minutes! She looked like she had been wrung out like a wash cloth.

I was confident that there were demons present who were now vulnerable and stripped of their rights, so I told them we would try it one more time. I bound them up in the name of Jesus and commanded a demon prince to identify himself. Immediately she heard something but she seemed to hesitate as if unwilling to confess what she heard. The demon did not speak through my sister's mouth. When he spoke only she could hear what he said. I told her that was the most common way and that she would have to tell me what she heard.

Finally, she admitted that she heard "schizophrenia" but that it did not make sense to her because she had no known mental problems. I reminded her that our father had that one too. My thoughts were that she must have kept him at bay with her faithfulness to the Lord. I was sure that the prince demon and his kingdom of schizophrenia that was now before me stripped of their rights was the same crew that passed down from my father and had tortured and tormented him up to his death. It was with great pleasure that I was given the honor of commanding them directly into the pit in Jesus' name. That one was for my sister and my father. Praise be to God that the spirit of Schizophrenia was removed from my family tree.

I had a lot to think about on the forty minute drive home. Anytime God shows up and does miracles in your presence it is breathtaking, but this was double special. I was thrilled to see my sister get a new measure of freedom by following the example of Christ and deal with those who had severely tormented my father to the point of death. This represented much needed closure. Many times I wished I could have helped him. It was way too late for that, but God had just given me the opportunity to avenge him by removing the curse of schizophrenia from my family genetics. Yes, Jesus had become a curse for us so that the generational curses could be stopped in his mighty name. My sister received great freedom that night and of course I was thrilled to be a part of God's miracle for her, but I cannot adequately explain how good it made me feel to send those who had tormented my father into the pit never again to return in Jesus' name.

To date I have been a part of many miraculous experiences, yet this one was more special than all the rest, and yet I almost refused to go. I nearly let my pride and ego talk me out of receiving this awesome present from God. At the time I was totally oblivious as to the blessings that were in store for me. Even though I felt that my time had been disrespected that day, I chose to go anyway with a humble heart, and how great was my reward!

The lessons I was taught by this experience were of immeasurable value. God was telling my sister that she was only His servant and requiring that she forgive everyone. This was also the main understanding that I took home. This was the same battle that I was fighting as I considered if I would go minister at my sister's beck and call or if I would refuse because I had been disrespected. Jesus said it plainly that greatest among us was servant of all and there is no room for pride or ego in someone who is called to serve everyone in humility. A servant or slave has no rights to defend. All such rights go to the slave owner. When we defer our rights to Him, who has bought us and commands us to follow his example of unconditional love and forgiveness, then and only then will we experience true freedom and happiness. I would have to remember how close I was to missing out on the greatest blessing of my life and do my best to stay humble.

Another Miracle for Sandy

January 3, 2010 — On this Sunday morning, I awoke with some good news for Sandy. I had received a message from God, who had said He wanted to complete some more work inside her. I was trying to gently say that she had more demons that he wanted to free her from. The news was not well received. As a matter of fact, she snapped back at me for suggesting such. Who did I think I was going around always accusing people of having demons? If anyone could be relied upon to have respect for my ministry at this point I thought it was her, but she totally rebuffed me and was insulted. I was hurt and surprised because what I was telling her was that God wanted to do another miracle for her, and only God knew what good things might come from it. My pride started to swell as I became instantly irritated. In times past I would have laid into her for such insolence but instead of trying to put her in her place, I did something that was very much out of character for me. I repressed my anger, told her to have fun with them, and walked away—putting her into the Lord's hands.

From that day forward, I knew it would not be easy to help people understand that the chances were good that they had demonic bondage which was causing them all sorts of unnecessary hardships that they could be free from if they would face the reality of God's Word and act on it. The propaganda war waged by the forces of darkness regarding themselves has been so intense that it is difficult for anyone to process information that they could have a demon without responding just like Sandy. She was ready to be done with the whole thing, and I get that, but she had already tasted the good things that came from deliverance, and if God wanted to do another miracle for her, she should have thought it through to the end to know it was truly great news. To think that we might have a demon is scary and unpleasant, but the reality is that Christians are living with all sorts of problems that Christ has paid for us to be free from if only they would embrace the truth of God's Word and find freedom. Demons cause us problems whether they are inside or outside, but once inside they put us in bondage and may cause a host of diseases and disorders. I believe that our salvation can remain intact with some lower level bondage to demons but the reality is that we should not put up with them, and any form of demonic bondage makes us especially vulnerable to more. Their intent is to make our lives miserable, and their presence greatly increases our chances of falling away. The bottom line is that when demons are attached we have a curse on us that weighs us down and trips us up when we should be running the race effortlessly in freedom.

The best analogy that I can think of to compare what it looks like for a demon to be in someone is to have an external hard drive connected to a computer. This external drive, or demon, connects to the system and unleashes harmful programs designed to disrupt, steal data, install all sorts of malicious software that will make the computer work slowly and poorly, and shut down the internet connection (communication to God). Demons basically do the same thing when connected to us. All of the sudden, we cannot concentrate on important tasks in favor of doing things that are irrelevant. We become generally unproductive and sick. Simply put, our minds are messed up and we are no longer in control. We do not do what we want and need to be doing, and all sorts of negative consequences arise. Our tendency is to blame the effects of the curse on "bad luck" or bad genetics instead of focusing on the root cause of the problems that seem to randomly happen to us.

When a computer is infected, the malicious software attempts to work behind the scenes so it can do all the damage it can to the operating system before being detected. Unfortunately, most people who come for deliverance have tried all other medical options and are desperate because their systems have been completely hijacked and are out of control. Jesus has given us the ultimate ability to clean our systems from all the malicious software that has invaded us and keep us clean and running at peak performance.

Four days after giving Sandy her good, but received as bad, news, she was at my house and we were preparing to watch Alabama play Texas in the BCS national championship football game. It was just the two of us. Alabama football was a big deal for her, and all of our friends joined us for the big game. I enjoyed seeing Bama win but for Sandy—a win meant the world would be a much happier place for several days. With that in mind, I was pulling for the Tide.

Just before kickoff Sandy did something that was very odd. She pressed record on the DVR, turned off the TV, and asked if we could talk. For her to put something ahead of the game, I knew it must be serious, so she had my full attention. She explained that ever since I had given her the message about God having more freedom for her, she had been having headaches and had been generally uncomfortable. The headaches had become so intense of late that she could hardly function. She shared that God had revealed a few more people over the last few days that she needed to forgive and that all of them were women. So, she decided that she wanted more ministry after all.

This was no occasion to say, "I told you so" because this woman was in physical pain. Immediately I commanded all demons inside that temple of the Holy Spirit to be bound in the name of Jesus. I told Sandy to confess with her mouth that nobody owed her anything and that she was only God's servant. I directed her to confess that she had completely forgiven and released all the people God had shown her one at a time. I then commanded a prince demon to identify himself. As before a demon spoke up and identified himself as "the gatekeeper." I learned about this type in the Dickerman book but had never encountered one before. A gatekeeper demon is one whose assignment is to coordinate and facilitate the flow of new demonic entrants into the host. He is a top tier administrator of sorts who determines when God's rules allow for more entrants and who the new entrants are. When a demonic stronghold is under attack through deliverance ministry, the lower ranks are forced to answer first so this type is usually one of the last to be extracted. With his permissions stripped away by

Sandy's willingness to forgive, the demon left just as easily as the others in the name of Jesus.

After commanding another prince demon to identify himself, I was surprised when Sandy burst out laughing. I mean she laughed so hard and continuously that it upset me momentarily. It was as if she was laughing at me. I studied her and surmised that it was just another attempt of the demon trying to avoid extraction with theatrics. I bound him again in Jesus name and told him there would be no more of that monkey business and again commanded him to identify himself. He then offered that he was, "I am." Further conversation revealed that he was the top demon in charge over all the other kingdoms. The very nerve of this vain demon to claim God's name! He paid the price for his vanity as his entire kingdom was destroyed and his rights stripped away when Sandy adopted proper attitude toward the Lord and others. When I commanded the demon out, his exit came just as easy as the rest. Just like that, Sandy was a totally free woman. After a few minutes of recovering her faculties, she was feeling better than ever. Interestingly, this day was the last of her week long fast. The icing on the cake was that we were able to skip through the commercials to see Bama win yet another championship.

It was clear that God was helping me understand and training me to provide proper ministry through these initial experiences with close friends and family. I was learning to lean on Him throughout the process and that this was not necessarily a "one and done" situation. Scripture supports that all believers are "justified" when they commit to the Lord but then go through a "sanctification" process.

When someone has been playing host to demonic kingdoms for long periods of time, the person wrongly associates his or her identity with the evil tendencies of the demonic kingdoms. For example, let's say that a person has bondage in the area of food and career. This person cannot finish one meal before becoming overwhelmed with concern for the next one. He cannot think of taking time off from work because he is just too important and too busy. If this person gives his life to God, God has some work to do in both of these areas but only He knows exactly how fast the person can handle it and He will not allow His subjects to be overwhelmed. The biblical precedent for this teaching is found in Exodus 23:

> [27] I will send my fear before thee, and will destroy all the people to whom thou shalt come, and I will make all thine enemies turn their backs unto thee.
>
> [28] And I will send hornets before thee, which shall drive out the Hivite, the Canaanite, and the Hittite, from before thee.
>
> [29] I will not drive them out from before thee in one year; lest the land become desolate, and the beast of the field multiply against thee.
>
> [30] By little and little I will drive them out from before thee, until thou be increased, and inherit the land.

This sentiment is also reiterated in Deuteronomy 7:21-23. It does not take much insight into the symbolism in Deuteronomy 7 to see that this entire chapter is a strong message to the modern believer regarding deliverance and freedom from our spiritual enemies.

January 19, 2010 — This was the day that Sandy had an appointment with her OBGYN, Dr. Samuel Gray, for a re-check to confirm her healing. After my mind-blowing experiences the night that I commanded the spirit of cancer to leave her, I had no doubt that she was healed, but Sandy had not seen everything I had. Even so she knew something had happened. She exercised her faith and was diligent to follow the instructions that were given to me for her.

Sandy called me as she left the Brookwood Medical Center with the news. She said she announced to all the staff and the doctor that she believed that God had healed her and that she was just there for confirmation. She reported that all the staff seemed to completely ignore her statements as if she was just some religious fruitcake. When her exam showed that there was nothing wrong with her, they continued to ignore her explanation. The proof was there, but her doctor remained confused and only looked for other reasons as to why he could not find any of the conditions he saw on her last visit. Determined to refute Sandy's explanation of her renewed health, he offered that they could have made a mistake, and that lab work would be necessary to confirm that she truly was in good health. Once again, Sandy insisted that they had not made a mistake because she knew that God healed her. With that the doctor finally conceded that miracles do happen and that they would call her in a few days with the results of the lab test.

January 22, 2010 — Things had been quiet lately regarding my divorce suit, but with just one week before it was set to go to trial, my attorneys, Lisa Woods and Steve Wright, requested that we meet at Steve's Najjar Denaburg Law office in Birmingham for a refresher.

It had taken three years of litigation to get to this point, and there is no telling how many cases had come and gone for these counselors since they took mine. We had multiple judges followed by as many recusals. There were multiple court-ordered mediations followed by as many failures. My girls even had their own court ordered attorney, the "guardian ad litem," whose fees I had to pay half of. An independent accounting firm in Montgomery had been hired to put a value on my company. I had my own expert accountant on the payroll. It was a legal circus, and I was the clown stuck with the bill.

Wonderful, we had a trial date that was set for January 28, 2010, but I had long since learned to avoid pinning too much hope on any sort of resolution. By design, if a couple forces the court system to sort through their dirty laundry, the court will make sure that neither side wins. In nasty divorces like mine, even after a court ruling, closure is hard to achieve when there are always other opportunities for appeals and other such legal wranglings designed to continue the attack promoted by unscrupulous attorneys looking to churn more fees. Over the last three years, I had seen trial dates come and go every three to four months. With continuance after continuance, I wondered if I would ever be divorced.

I had great respect for my attorneys. Aside from being very talented and respected among their peers, it was clear that they worked very well together and had a sincere interest in helping me. Lisa was not old enough to be my mother but because of the kind but stern motherly direction she had given me over the years, I had come to refer to her affectionately as "Moma." Mr. Wright, on the other hand was an older gentleman who exuded an heir of intelligence and experience that commanded respect. In one of our early court appearances, I gained a whole new level of appreciation for him when one of the judges called him to the bench to ask his opinion on an unrelated matter. I thought to myself, "Did the judge really ask my lawyer for help in understanding the law?"

I knew that it was not their fault that my legal matter had not been resolved. Yes, it had been my refusal to submit to God. As I drove to the meeting, I pondered how I would give them the news.

A few weeks prior, I was sitting alone at home when I got a clear command from God. He told me that I was not to tell a single lie in the courtroom. I had been reading my Bible a lot lately and my mind was fresh on just how important the truth was to God. I knew that He was the Way, the Truth and the Life. I knew that

He hated false witness. I knew that Jesus said that lies were the native language of the devil. His command was clear and I would not disobey. I had to level with my attorneys about the new rules and plan.

A week before trial, my attorneys were trying to refresh their minds as to two versions of the truth. They knew what really happened and were trying to tweak an alternative version that we wanted everyone else to believe but over time important details and strategies have to be refreshed. The main purpose of our meeting was to make sure we had our stories straight. Much of our legal strategy hinged on a little massaging of the truth here and there and in the case of my affair, an outright denial of any misconduct prior to separation. Many hours of preparation and planning over the last few years had gone into what my attorneys believed would be the best image of me to present to the court. These attorneys had built their law practices and reputations on winning good verdicts or settlements for their clients and they were very competitive and serious about maintaining their record. To let the other side beat them was not acceptable and they would work hard to prevent it. They did not know it yet but all their well laid plans for victory were out the window.

When I arrived at Mr. Wright's office, Lisa was already there and within a few minutes the three of us were seated in a conference room. I decided that I would drop the bomb early. As soon as we exchanged the customary pleasantries, I announced to them that there was a change of plans. I would not be telling a single lie in the courtroom. My announcement hit them hard, as their jaws nearly hit the table. Mr. Wright was the first to recover and respond by saying that in their professional opinion, they could not advise that I do that.

I went on to explain how I had made some big changes in my relationship with God, and He had been doing some miraculous things, and that this was from Him. Sensing my resolve they asked me to excuse myself to the lobby so they could confer privately with Audra's attorney on a few other issues. While standing in the lobby, as if on cue, my cell rang. It was Sandy saying that her doctor's office had just called and that her lab work proved that she was in perfect health. All alone in this upstairs lobby, I did a little victory jig praising God for what He had done. It was like God was telling me, "Yes, I have this too." When the door opened and I was invited back in, I was all the more fired up about doing what God said at trial and I told them about Sandy's healing. Both seemed to be struck by my witness and not sure what to think about the changed person who sat before them.

Divorce Court

January 28, 2010 — This was the first day of my divorce trial at the Tuscaloosa County courthouse. I was not sure what to expect, but I knew in my heart that God was with me. I had been on a Daniel fast since Dec 30th, and my faith had grown to expect a miracle. I felt sure that something was going to happen one way or another.

All the family court judges in Tuscaloosa County had recused themselves from handling my case which forced judicial authorities in Montgomery to nominate a replacement from another district. The honorable Judge Dawn Hare from Monroeville was chosen. My attorneys were encouraged because nobody around here had much experience with her, and they knew of no political connections that might create the kind of complications we had been experiencing.

Monroeville, is a small town in south Alabama where timber products are a large part of the local economy. Judge Hare's district was home to a large veneer and plywood company which had recently closed due to the horrible housing market. Many families in her district were suffering due to job losses. Before the start of the trial, Judge Hare laid out a few ground rules and offered clues as to her viewpoint and she mentioned that several businesses had closed in her district and that she would not have a hard time being convinced that similar businesses were under similar duress. All I could do was praise God under my breath as I watched Audra and her lawyers let her comments sink in.

The trial finally began with Audra being put on the witness stand so she could answer questions chosen by her attorney. Nothing was ever mentioned about the affair or anything like that but let's just say nothing good was said about me. All I did was sit quietly in the corner, listening and praying. Finally, Lisa was given the opportunity to cross examine. I could tell it was going to be entertaining, but just as she got started, somebody pushed the pause button and told us to come back the next day. The epitome of inefficiency, after backing out the long lunch break, the total amount of time in trial for the whole day was only about 4 hours.

The following day began just like the previous one ended. Audra was on the stand with Moma Lisa cross examining. Lisa was stomping around and got so wound up that I thought she might punch her stilettos right through the tile floor. I had never seen this side of Moma Lisa. My memory flashed back to comments Bill McGuire said about her when he recommended her to me. He said she would make you think she was going to claw your eyeballs out with her fingernails. While her courtroom posture was somewhat imposing, it was her quick wit and well-organized questions, which were supported by impeccable memory of the facts, that did the most damage. She poked holes and prodded Audra's testimony such that Audra was clearly uncomfortable and squirming in her chair. Lisa was tearing into her witness with such vigor that at one point the judge interrupted her and warned her to tone it down. It had gotten so ugly that, even after all Audra had put me through, I began to feel sorry for her. After about an hour of that, Audra meekly looked to the judge and asked for a break. Her honor agreed and before I knew it, Audra asked if we could talk privately in the hall just outside the courtroom. For the first time ever, she seemed motivated to settle the case. I had to be careful to conceal my enthusiasm because as badly as I wanted to end it, I needed to negotiate for something I could afford, and the reality was that I was flat broke and going deeper in debt every day. We somehow agreed to rough numbers and by the end of the day all the details were hashed out. Delighted to see us resolve the matter without her having to hand down a decision, Judge Hare oversaw the closing of the settlement. In the courtroom with the stenographer tapping away, the agreement was read into the record, signed and witnessed with both parties in agreement. My attorneys were overjoyed with the outcome. They had feared for what would come of my case because they knew I would tell the truth on the witness stand but I never even had to answer one question. It was a miracle!

It was over. Was it over? As my attorneys offered congratulations, I heard Audra call my name from the other side of the courtroom with a look of desperation on her face. She said she forgot to ask for the club membership. I told her not to worry about it and that she could have that too.

February – April 2010 — During this time, God continued to amaze with opportunities to help friends and family get free from all sorts of demonic bondage. Powerful ministry opportunities contrasted greatly with my failing business. I was asking God why he was showing me his power and yet withholding financial healing.

Settler's Regret

I knew Audra, and my gut told me that she would have second thoughts about our deal. She was scrambling for more even before leaving the courtroom and I suspected there was more, maybe much more that she had forgotten to demand in our settlement and by now hated our deal. Rumors would soon spread that Audra's father was livid because my payment of her legal fees had not been addressed in the settlement. The story was that she owed her lawyers for all the legal work done on her behalf since the beginning. I guess Audra's threat of hiring the best lawyers my money could buy did not work out so well for her in the end. I shared my concern that Audra would renege, but my lawyers said there was not much else that she could do because we had a signed agreement and the judge was a witness.

The next step would be for our agreement to be formalized and re-written into a proper document called a Final Judgement of Divorce or FJD. Once both sides agreed that the re-write was representative of the agreement, the final product would be provided to the judge for her signature and filing before it would become the Final Judgement of Divorce. This should have taken no more than a week or two, but as suspected Audra would not allow her attorneys to accept the formal document.

Audra's rub was that a big chunk of her settlement was to come from the equity in our home. The problem was that it had to be sold and sold for enough before she got her money. We were in the height of the housing crisis and jumbo homes were just not selling unless the buyer had cash. She knew the chances of selling our home was not good, and she got squirrely.

May 3, 2010 — Amid rumors that Audra was planning to take legal action aimed at backing out of our deal, Judge Hare decided to move forward anyway and sign the FJD. I was finally divorced!

May 10, 2010—Sandy and I were married on a public beach in Destin, Florida. In attendance, there was a preacher, photographer, and three old ladies who happened to be seated in the area when we got there. We were happy to have them and their kind compliments of how handsome a couple we made. I am sure there was a great cloud of witnesses there also, and I can't wait to find out who else was there one day.

Back when God commanded me to tell nothing but the truth in the courtroom, he also gave me another equally disconcerting instruction. When I married Sandy, it would be without a pre-nuptial agreement. During all the divorce Hell that I had been through, I loathed the control that my wife exerted over me. I took all the money that I saved prior to our marriage and bought Cahaba Veneer shortly after we married, and yet she believed herself entitled to more than it was worth. The bottom line is that all the wealth that had been accumulated during the course of our marriage was from me and she did little more than deplete it. The whole time that I was being brutalized in the legal system, I groaned and lamented that I did not have a pre-nuptial agreement to protect me from this unreasonable woman. I swore the whole time that I was dealing with her that I would never marry again without one. I even asked my younger brother to have lunch with me and Lisa so she could counsel him on getting one should he ever think of getting married. All of that came to nothing when God told me that there would be no pre-nuptial agreement with Sandy. I was to trust Him and Him alone for protection.

May 28, 2010 — Audra's attorney filed a "Motion to Alter, Amend or Vacate." Refusing to leave well enough alone, Audra sought more legal action to change the terms of our settlement agreement signed back on January 29th. This woman simply would not be satisfied until the house sold or she got her money. It had gotten to the point that my faith was stronger to believe for supernatural healing and deliverance than for her harassment to end.

SOLD!

While costly houses such as the one we needed to sell were just not moving, I badly needed to divest of mine to pay my ex-wife and get her off my back. Shortly after we settled, our house was not yet listed when suddenly an interested prospect came forward. One of the neighbors heard our house would be on the market soon and told her new friend, Christina Grant. Christina and her husband Anthony were new to the area and were renting another home in the neighborhood until they could find a more permanent place. Anthony Grant or Coach Anthony Grant had just moved his family to Tuscaloosa to take the head basketball coaching position at the University of Alabama.

June 11, 2010 — Of all the houses Christina had to pick from in Tuscaloosa County, she fell in love with mine and paid just enough for it that I could pay off the bank and cover my obligation to Audra.

Learning to Trust Him

When I recently started studying the Bible with real purpose, I realized that I had never paid much attention to the Old Testament. To me it had always been sort of outdated and irrelevant. I mean after all, we now have the New Covenant. However, with God's call on my life such as it was, I decided it was past time that I take the entire body of God's Word seriously. As I read, God began to show me how the Old and New Testament scriptures rely upon one other for complete biblical understandings. As I read about the great exodus of the Israelites from Egypt, I recognized that they were an example for me right then. While God had resolved my divorce, set me free, and set my new wife free, my business and personal finances were still in a dry and barren place. God showed me that he was training me to trust him for my daily bread in the desert. Week in, week out God went before and behind me performing miracle after miracle, yet I could not get ahead financially. I had everything I needed to eat, and I was surviving, but I could not see any light in the tunnel and at times it would grow even darker. My mother's prophesy said that money would come, so I believed that God would eventually turn the tide, but it sure was hard to be patient with all signs suggesting otherwise.

On May 28th, the same day that Audra filed her last motion in an attempt to modify our settlement, my largest customer announced that they would not be buying any more veneer for a while because they were going to be able to supply themselves from an in house plant that they were starting back up. This was a tremendous blow that I wondered how I would recover from. We did not have many logs, and those we did have we could not pay for timely. My company was insolvent and I was impatiently stomping the ground in need of God to make some water flow.

Suddenly I had a new appreciation for what those Israelites faced as they followed God around the desert. A desert in not a happy place. Nothing grows there. There is little water or fodder for your livestock. The food gets old, and there are enemies who seek to block your way and cast curses on you. When that doesn't work, they will tempt you to sin. I was in the same fix as the Israelites were. I knew God was with me. I knew He was bigger than any of my predicaments, but my senses and bank account kept telling me a different story. The lesson of the Israelites helped me immensely. I kept telling God, "I don't know how you are going to do it, but I know you are going to do it. I am not going to be like those Israelites who saw your miracles but refused to trust you." I had to confess it over and over day after day because the stroll through the desert was brutal and would not be over soon.

The more I thought about it, who was I to demand anything from God? I did not go broke overnight, so who was I to think God would restore me overnight? I thank God for the Casting Crowns song "Praise You In the Storm" because many days it helped me maintain resolve to trust Him.

Collateral Repairs

Jesus set the precedent. 1 John 3:8 says that the Son of God was manifest that He might destroy the works of the devil. The record of Jesus' ministry is replete with examples of Jesus casting out demons with evidence of some sort of mental or physical healing.

With new found freedom, Sandy was exploring her new, real identity. After the first night of freedom, when she started eating ice cream, she confessed a habit that I was unaware of. She had been secretly throwing back a couple shots of tequila right when she got home from work. She hated smoking, had never done drugs and, with the exception of tequila, was not tempted by any other form of alcohol. I knew she had a particular affinity for margaritas, but I had no idea of the extent of this crutch. From the first night that she experienced freedom, her tequila habit was completely erased and she told me about it. It was blatantly obvious that when the demons left, they took it with them. I am not one who believes an alcoholic beverage is essentially evil, but like most everything else, it can easily become an idol and result in demonic problems. I believe Jesus turned water into wine and that God created this alcoholic beverage. He drank it at the Lord's Supper and shared that he would not drink it again until he was in heaven. That said, alcohol must be treated with caution like all other things that we humans tend to like a lot so that it does not become something that we love too much.

I am not suggesting that every human ailment is demonic, but I can say with 100% confidence that many people report relief from minor and major mental and physical abnormalities following successful deliverance.

The War on Freedom

There are many reasons why the mere thought of demons or deliverance is repulsive to most people, but there is one that is at the heart of them all. It is because that is how our enemies want it. Demons are like professional poker players. They are at the table and they have skin in the game. They far exceed us in skill and expertise. The challenge for them is that true believers are playing with an unbeatable hand. So, what do they do to beat us? They bluff. It matters not how good your hand is if you are too scared or do not know how to play it.

All of Hell works overtime to promote fear of themselves in the heart of man. They want us to think that interaction with them is uncommon and spooky. They want the subject of themselves to be taboo and generally inappropriate. Under those conditions, chances are slim that anyone will be confronting or taking authority over them in Jesus' name. It is easy to recognize that an elaborate propaganda campaign has been mounted on our culture. Their obvious design is to keep the kingdom of darkness firmly in charge through fear. There are tons of horror flicks that promote fear of evil spirits. Churches rarely touch on this sensitive and delicate subject. When they do teach on "spiritual warfare," many say it is best to avoid confrontation. How convenient.

The Bible teaches that Satan and his demons suffered a decisive defeat at the hands of Jesus (Col 2:15) and that Jesus shared his victory/authority over them with us (Luke 10:19). Given

Christ's victory and allocation of authority to His followers, it should be most troubling that Satan has so effectively managed to maintain his kingdom of evil throughout the world. Something has gone awry.

The stark reality is that many people, including Christians are under the influence of a demon or demons but have no clue. The cleverness of these creatures should never be discounted and the fact that they are so successful is a testament to their resourcefulness. In my opinion, C.S. Lewis, in his classic *The Screwtape Letters*, gives us a reasonably good idea of what their activities look like. Their assignment is precarious, to say the least, considering that Jesus has already come to the world and given us everything we need to trample them. Even still, multitudes of believers are unnecessarily killed, stolen from, and destroyed while completely oblivious to the cause and that they hold the power to stop it in Jesus' name. If people know that demons are causing their problems, chances dramatically increase that they will buy the right book, or talk to the right minister, or maybe even sign up for a Freedom small group with Church of the Highlands.

Christians with Demons

Many believers have been duped with the notion that they are immune to demons. Our spiritual enemies gain much advantage from the acceptance of this lie. My ministry is not to unbelievers but to those who profess Jesus as Lord or are willing to do so. It would be pointless to minister to those who have no basis for freedom. God is the one who sets the rules regarding demonic access and we must refer to His Word for authority on this subject and reject the self-aggrandizing lies peddled by the enemy. Even the apostle Paul was not immune, as God allowed a demon to irritate him in the interest of keeping him humble. (2 Corinthians 12:7)

My experience with ministering to my wife has taught me volumes on this subject. Sandy is an introverted, quiet, and very sensitive person. Over the years I have watched closely over her progress as she has learned her new identity in Christ Jesus. From the time that she was completely free until now, there have been at least half a dozen times that she has let a demon back in. For the most part, it was because of unforgiveness. Somebody hurt her, and she could not let it go. When you have been branded with the scarlet letter in a small community such as ours, there will be many opportunities to get your feelings hurt. In Matthew 18:34, Jesus tells us that we will be turned over to the tormentors unless we continue to walk in forgiveness toward others just as God forgives us. Regardless of what someone does to us or someone close to us, we must forgive them from our hearts or else we open the door up to the devil to get a foothold. We must also forgive ourselves or else the same rule applies. We must adopt a spirit of unconditional love and forgiveness toward everyone including ourselves such that nobody owes us anything. Period.

I will not sugar coat what this means. If you sincerely profess Jesus as your Lord and have asked God to forgive you, and you hold offence toward anyone, you have a demon or demons. My experience is that as soon as you decide how you will handle the offense, if it does not involve forgiveness, a demon will come into you and the problems will begin.

When this happened to Sandy, I could sense it by immediate changes in her behavior, attitude or physical complaints. Again, the demon would not be outright obvious as to his presence, but because I was so attentive and knew her so well I could tell when things were not right.

A Tip from God—Handling Offense

When people hurt us, there is always a period of time where we mull over how we will respond. This period of deliberation will lead to either an open or closed door to the enemy. Sandy continued to struggle to forgive until she finally broke down and prayed to God for help. She knew what she was supposed to do but somehow could not consistently perform, which resulted in a recurring cycle of offense, demonic oppression, and ministry from me. She said that God gave her a simple tip that fixed the problem. He told her to just keep talking to Him about it until she was over it. Praying is talking to God, so instead of talking to anyone else, just pray and vent on God. It is not gossiping if you are telling God all about it, and He wants to hear from us and for us to place all our burdens on Him. Anytime you are tempted to think negative thoughts, pray/talk to God about it and do not stop until He gives you peace in your heart to turn the whole matter over and let Him handle it. Try to avoid being all religious as you talk to God. Talk to Him just like you would your best friend who cares about you. Talk to Him like He is the kind of friend who can truly heal the hurt deep within you and turn your sadness into joy.

Demons from Intentional Disobedience

When we make Jesus our Lord, it means we make Him our boss. When we refuse to follow directions from the boss, this is sin, and this can result in demonic access. Often times, God corrects us with demonic torment when we refuse to obey.

The Bible teaches that there are two types of sin, "intentional" and "unintentional." (Num. 15:22-36) When we make an honest mistake, repent, and set our hearts against future offenses, it is unintentional sin. As an employer, I will work with employees who make honest mistakes with the understanding that they will do their best to not let it happen again. I will have no choice but to fire someone who intentionally and repeatedly refuses to follow company policy. When we know better and we continue in sin with unrepentant hearts, then we are opening the door to demonic torment. Old Testament scripture indicates the atonement sacrifices offered by priests on behalf of the sins of the people would cover only unintentional sin. We would be wise to apply this understanding to our present situation as we deal with what God points out as sin in our lives.

Don't be fooled by people talking about how Jesus has covered all our past, present, and future sins when the reality is that once we make Jesus Lord, our present and future sins must be unintentional and honest mistakes or else Jesus is not truly Lord. We must not be foolish enough to think that Jesus' sacrifice was done to allow us to continue intentionally sinning going forward. Intentional sin is tantamount to rebellion.

I will never forget one instance of a lady who I had once already led through deliverance. The first meeting was highly successful, but about nine months later we spoke by phone, and she asked me to minister to her again. When I got to her house to meet with her and her husband, she explained that though she had experienced a great deal of freedom, something was not quite right. After hours of getting nowhere, I finally asked God to show us what it was. Thankfully, God told her, again. He said He told her to stop drinking alcohol, and she had refused. She claimed that she did not get drunk, and she just wanted to have a few social drinks. She had told God no but when she agreed to obey, a demon finally was forced to come forward and identify himself and was cast out. There was one more. While in college at the University of Alabama this distinguished woman was president of Chi Omega sorority. She had been very proud of this and refused to obey God when he told her to cut all ties with her sorority as she continued to write recommendations for girls going through rush. She explained to me that God was not happy with Chi Omega because of a blasphemous skit performed during initiation. The intent of the performance was to draw a comparison between the transition of pledges to active member status and Jesus rising from the dead. I was shocked that anyone would dare treat the raising of Christ from the dead with such trivial contempt. I counseled her to obey God by repenting of all ties to her sorority and after doing so, the demon identified himself and left in the name of Jesus. As I spoke the command she said she could see her son's mind clearing as he sat in his classroom.

I later got further confirmation of God's disdain for the practices of Chi Omega sorority when I read *Invisible Enemies* by Jim Croft. In his book, Jim gives an account of serious demonic disturbances which were determined to be the result of connections to this poplar sorority.

Back to Business

Even as I continued to see evidence of God's power manifest in exciting ministry opportunities, Cahaba Veneer was hanging on by a mere thread. My business was bleeding so badly that I wondered if it was God's will for it to survive. I did not care so much about money anymore, but I did have a lot of obligations such as child support and the settlement that I promised to pay my ex-wife over the next seven years. Even with all these bills, I knew God could provide by other means if that was His choice and if something did not change soon, His choice would be obvious.

I talked to my attorneys, Lisa and Steve, and told them of my concerns. Steve set up an appointment with one of his partners at Najjar Denaburg to discuss what bankruptcy might look like. Sandy and I drove to Birmingham for the meeting. As I drove home, I knew that failure was not an option. There was just no way that I could see bankruptcy as part of God's plan because it would mean utter devastation for all involved, and I began to fervently pray for God to save my company.

God Checks In

As if to let me know He was still holding the universe in His hands, God sent me a signal that He was still with me. As had become His preferred method, His modus operandi was to go through my mother. I hate to admit it but I was very slow to recognize and give proper deference to my mother relative to her spiritual gifts and in particular as a spokeswoman for God. At this point, I had fully caught on. Never again would she speak and her words go in one ear and out the other. She had my full attention, and I would never be too busy again to take her calls.

September 23, 2010 — Mother called to say hello and see how I was doing. Toward the end of the call, she mentioned that I should consider going to a meeting at Rod Wilkin's home. I asked her if it was one of those God suggestions or just a suggestion and she said she was not sure. I decided that I would go to make sure.

At this time, Mr. Wilkin was in the habit of having Delores Winder come to speak and pray for people at his home. Rod's priorities changed some years ago when late stage melanoma was found lodged into his back. He was being treated at UAB Medical Center in Birmingham and was told that there was nothing they could do to treat the aggressive cancer and that he should get his affairs in order because it would soon take his life. When God responded to his request and healed him, it had become his mission to promote God and his healing power for others.

When I drove to the meeting later that night, I did not know anything much about the guest speaker or Mr. Wilkin. As far as I knew, it was just some sort of prayer meeting. When I got to the Wilkin's neighborhood, I was impressed with the long line of cars parked down the street. When I got to the house, the living room and foyer were filled with people and had been converted into a sort of church sanctuary with all the furniture removed and replaced with folding chairs arranged in rows. There was a table displaying books written by Delores Winder and as I visited with other guests, I learned that Mrs. Winder was well known for a dynamic healing ministry which followed her own miraculous healing experience. I would soon learn that Mrs. Winder was no ordinary woman of God.

All of this was great, but I was trying to understand why I was there. The meeting began with praise and worship, followed by a brief message from Mrs. Winder, which was then followed by prayers for healing. When Mrs. Winder began speaking, I could hardly believe it, but her message was about forgiveness and deliverance. Everything she said resonated with me such that I was ready to jump out of my seat. At the end of her message, she closed her eyes and said that she sensed someone with this or that problem and that God was touching them. It appeared that she actually felt their pain as God revealed it to her and she spoke healing over them.

At the end of the service, I was standing around waiting to see if I would have the chance to meet Mrs. Winder but she was completely surrounded. Her visits to Tuscaloosa had become well known and people in need of healing traveled long distances in hope that God might touch them through her anointing. People were asking for prayer, saying hello and buzzing all around. I was just about to give up when she reached through the crowd, grabbed my arm, pulled me to the side and sat me down into one of the chairs to talk privately as if we were best friends. After introducing myself, she kept saying, "You are a minister aren't you? You are in ministry, right?" Confused, having never laid eyes on her before in my life, I assumed she mistook me for a pastor or other type of church leader. I told her, "No ma'am, I am a business owner." She would have none of it and kept pressing me. Finally she said, "I know you are in ministry." It finally hit me. Somehow, she knew that I was called into the deliverance ministry. Once I understood I joyfully said yes and that I was called into the deliverance ministry. I was amazed that this little lady knew stuff about me that she was not supposed to just like my mother. As far as I knew, nobody at the meeting had a clue about God's call on my life. I was impressed with her gifts and could barely contain my joy for being called out to this powerful woman of God. Before saying goodbye, she invited me to join her for a private meeting back at the Wilkin home in two days. Intrigued, I told her I would plan on it.

The meeting was on a Saturday and Sandy agreed to go with me. There were about ten people there who were already seated in the living room of the Wilkin home when we arrived. Mr. Wilkin welcomed us graciously and offered us a copy of the book that

Delores would be discussing and promoting that day. Sandy and I could hardly believe it when he offered us a copy of *When Pigs Move In* by Don Dickerman, and the purpose of the meeting was to discuss the deliverance ministry.

My Biggest Love Challenges

Even though I find it much easier than Sandy to let offenses roll off my back, I have had occasional challenges.

One of the biggest challenges that I was yet to face was Sandy's oldest daughter, who was just turning sixteen on October 19, 2010. I felt sure that she blamed me and her mom for all the pain that she endured relative to the divorce. Her father had done well to absolve himself of responsibility. The tension in my home when she was around was insufferable. She refused to look at or speak to me and if she did, I wished she had not. Nevertheless she was the daughter of the woman I loved, and I made it my mission to somehow make it work. No matter how hard I tried, she was unyielding and refused to so much as acknowledge my presence most of the time.

It all came to a head on Nov 24, 2010 when I left early in the morning to run some errands in Tuscaloosa. It was a sunny Saturday morning, and Sandy asked her daughter if she would like to go to Tuscaloosa to shop around and have lunch. She was overjoyed to have time with her mom without me around. At the last minute her mom told her that I was close by and would be joining them for lunch. In disgust, she initially refused to enter the restaurant. When I figured out what happened, I did not let on that it irritated me but after letting it simmer the rest of the day, I was boiling mad and let it all loose on her mother. I forbade her from giving her one more penny of support. Until recently she had lived with her dad exclusively but now that she needed a car, she was tolerating me until she got what she wanted, or at least that is what it seemed like to me. I knew I was supposed to love and forgive unconditionally, but her disrespect of me had crossed the line, and I would not allow it any longer. After all, I thought my reaction was fully justified because I had a duty as her stepparent and it would not be proper for me to allow this child to treat me with such disrespect.

Later that night, Sandy went to bed early without a word. She did not react with gesture or word to my rant. It was as if what I said struck her to the core and robbed her of strength. She understood my pain and her daughter's pain and loved us both. As for me I could not sleep. I just laid on my back, wide-eyed, thinking it over. I was unsure if I was handling things the way that God wanted me to. I remembered what Sandy had learned from God when she was offended and could not let it go so I resolved to just keep talking to God about it. I finally dozed off while praying and woke again a few hours later. At that point, I decided to move to the living room sofa. I got comfortable and dozed until the sun streamed through the open windows. Just as I woke I heard four words that instantly took away the offense and healed my heart toward my stepdaughter. I heard, "I died for you." What happened when He spoke was amazing. It was not just the message of the words but also the power that was in them to heal, convey understanding, and bring peace. I knew in that instant that I must forgive and take back all that I said the previous evening. As soon as Sandy was awake, I meekly recanted and asked her to forget all that I said the night before. It took time, but eventually the unconditional love that Sandy and I showed her daughter overcame her bitterness and our relationships were fully healed and restored. Love never fails.

By far the greatest love challenge that just keeps coming back is my ex-wife. After Audra and I finally divorced, it was clear that she continued to nurse grudges toward me and especially Sandy. Audra told me early on that she was fine with me dating anyone else but Sandy. Her hatred of Sandy was so intense that it seemed to me that one of the main reasons that Audra was refusing to divorce me was so that she could block our plans to be together.

As a result of her smear campaign, my name was so disgraced that my mother suggested I apologize to everyone in the family for having endured the shame of relation to me.

After the divorce, Audra would not stop looking for ways to hurt me. We had two children that I wanted to be there for and she would use them against me. From the time we separated, it was a constant battle for me to get the tiny amount of visitation with my children as ordered by the court. I was determined to have the minimal time of every other weekend with the girls even though it had become a constant battle of demanding my time and putting up with her dictating the schedule as suited her. I eventually had to sue her for failing to comply with visitation as ordered by the court. In an attempt to settle the dispute, it became abundantly clear just how much Audra despised my time with our children when she offered to forego the $3250 per month child support if I would agree to give up my rights to see them. Her offer was legitimized by the fact that she presented it through her attorney to mine! It was just another offensive insult to my integrity as a dedicated father. Times were tight, and it was a lot of money, but of course the answer was that no amount of money would convince me to walk away from my children.

Over and over again, Sandy and I exercised our "unconditional love" muscles and would forgive Audra for her repeated offenses. We knew the unsavory spiritual consequences if we did not. We also knew that Audra was highly offended, and what that said about her spiritual condition. Understanding this principle certainly sheds light on what Jesus meant when he said for us to pray for our enemies. We have been in no way perfect in our dealings with her but would eventually return to the safety of giving her over to the Lord and on occasion would find ourselves with sincere hearts praying for her freedom. Audra has heard much about my conversion and heart to serve the Lord but has refused to acknowledge any of it as legitimate. I have on several occasions tried to explain to her the importance of forgiveness and I believe that someday peace will come. Love never fails.

Darkest Right Before Dawn—June 2011

The contrast between my spiritual and financial health was never more obvious than it was in 2011.

My company had a million dollar line of credit that was maxed out and I had five hundred thousand dollars more of checks on my desk that were written but could not be released until more money came in. As customers paid me for product, Sandy would release as many payments to suppliers as she could only to add more to the stack every week. I used to daydream about the old days. The first ten years of my business I had a line of credit but had never used one dime of it. Our lack of money was a constant thorn in our sides. I had to tell her and myself continuously, "I don't know how He is going to do it, but I know He is going to do it."

As odd as it sounds, going to prison had become my escape. A medium security state prison was only about a mile from my plant. The spiritual needs of the Bibb County Correctional Facility were handled by Chaplain Maurice Lee. It had been on my mind to volunteer at the prison but did not know how to get involved. I got an introduction to Chaplain Lee or "Chap" after I agreed to unload two large air handlers which were delivering to the prison for the newly constructed prison chapel. Chap and I got along well from the start. When I approached him about volunteering, he said he would let me know when a position came open where I might serve. Shortly thereafter he called to say that an organization known as Prison Fellowship Ministries (PFM) was looking for a volunteer. Before long I was cleared to go into one of the dorms and teach basic Bible information to the inmates. For the most part, I was by myself in the company of hundreds of inmates during my work there but never felt threatened. My service was supervised by another PFM volunteer who was very strict with content that I was allowed to cover with the prisoners. The only time I got to ad lib was when the new PFM training materials did not arrive on time. The PFM material was great, but I longed to concentrate on my passion for freedom through forgiveness and repentance.

PFM was founded by the infamous and famous Chuck Colson. He was infamous early in career as the self-described "hatchet man" lawyer who served as "Special Counsel" to President Nixon. He was known as a "dirty tricks artist" but was highly respected as the shady but brilliant political strategist who laid the foundation for Nixon's 1972 landslide victory. He was convicted for obstruction of justice amidst the Watergate Scandal for trying to discredit one of Nixon's political enemies and served 7 months in a Federal prison. During Chuck's time in the slammer, he gave his heart to the Lord and started a Bible study in the prison. After his release, Chuck was convicted once again but this time by the Lord and the inmates who challenged him not to forget them as he went home and left them behind bars. Chuck would then become famous for starting what would become a $60,000,000 per year non-profit organization for the purpose of bringing the saving message of Christ to men behind bars.

The first year volunteering in the prison I was able to share my heart here and there as it fit into in the curriculum, but I was afraid that if I said anything about deliverance or demons that my conservative PFM supervisor would kick me to the curb. I grew bolder when mother called and said she thought my deliverance ministry would expand through my work at the prison. During this time, Chuck Colson was visiting Alabama to encourage staff and speak at some of the prisons where PFM operated. Out of nowhere I got an email invitation to eat breakfast with Chuck in Birmingham and decided to go. As we ate I boldly shared with him and the four other strangers my heart for deliverance. It was a strong first impression, but I had questions that I wanted him to answer, and this might be my only shot. I needed to know where he stood on the issue of the deliverance ministry because I did not want to serve under his banner if he did not approve. I was relieved when he said he believed in the merit of my ministry and that he supported my efforts. I knew I would have to be careful to avoid offending my supervisor, but as far as I was concerned, I had the support I needed from the very top and from that point forward I would not be denied.

The designed capacity of the Bibb County Correctional Facility is reportedly about one thousand men but the Alabama Department of Corrections somehow squeezed in closer to two. The men were grouped into separate dorms of a few hundred men each. The first thing that struck me was the total lack of privacy. Everything was wide open. All the bunk beds were in one large room and lots of glass in every wall to insure that nobody was out of sight, regardless of what you were doing. To get to my classroom I had to pass through the living quarters of the entire dorm. When passing through the center isle with a sea of bunks to the left and right toward the classroom in the back, I always tried my best to keep my eyes straight ahead so as to not further violate their privacy by looking at what little space these men called home.

In October 2011, it finally happened. At the end of one of my teaching sessions, an inmate named Donald Butler came forward and asked for prayer. I agreed. After all the other guys left the two of us in the classroom, I led him through a very successful session of deliverance. From that day forward, Donald became my right hand man. Unlike those I had ministered to in the free world, Donald was not ashamed to tell everyone in the dorm about the amazing freedoms that he now had and what God had done for him. I brought in a Dickerman book and he began to loan it to anyone interested. Donald was pushing others to read materials that I provided and seek freedom. Before I knew it, word was getting around. It became clear that my supervisor had heard about my extreme religious practices and was not excited about me being part of the team but he never straight up confronted me. I could just tell by the change in the way he treated me.

It was fine that my supervisor wanted me to go because I had other plans. After discussing with Chaplain Lee my concerns, he said I could use the new chapel one morning a week to speak to whoever in the prison wanted to come. This was a dream come true. I would not have to go through any dorms and I was not bound to discuss any particular curriculum. Donald went to work to promote the meeting and new faces were coming from various dorms to hear my teachings on love, forgiveness and freedom. I was bringing coffee and snacks to attract men to the meeting. One day after my meeting, I was ministering to one of the inmates on the front row of the chapel. I was quietly commanding demons out of this guy, but when they left he was coughing them out so loudly that Chaplain Lee thought he was getting sick or something so he bolted from the rear to see what was going on. When he got to us he was relieved to see that he was fine. Later on, I told him that he was just losing a few demons and he said he wondered as much and that he was a T.D. Jakes fan.

I was encouraged by Chaplain Lee's support. I asked if there was somewhere that I could meet with these men more privately for ministry, and he said I could use the conference room so he reserved it for "spiritual counseling" one day a week to meet with inmates who requested ministry. I was preaching one day a week and counseling another. I was ecstatic to be a part of what God was doing. I saw men delivered from all sorts of new demonic strongholds such as homosexuality and self-mutilation ("cutter"). I even saw one Hispanic guy get free from idol worship who was praying to a picture of Jesus that he kept tucked inside his Bible. He said that Jesus spoke to him and said that He did not look like that and to get rid of it. I had a sign-up sheet where inmates would put their name and ID # on a list and every week I would call for the next name on the list. I had a 2-3 month backlog of people waiting for a ministry, and I was content to take on the kingdom of darkness one person per week if that was what it took.

There was a flaw in my plan. Early in my prison experience I learned that volunteers were prime targets of con-artist prisoners who were constantly scheming for ways to use the sympathetic heart of the volunteer for their gain. Donald Butler had been asking me for money, but I resisted. After Donald was delivered, he and I spoke much more and I learned that he had no family outside the prison. Several other inmates confirmed that he didn't have anyone. I learned how hard it was to live among all the other men who regularly had family visits and got money deposited into their accounts. The inmates never saw real money but would get credit on their account which could be used to buy items like junk food, cigarettes, shoes and personal hygiene products. I learned how "favors" would have to be done to get stuff when you had no other means and that concerned me for Donald. I was convinced that Donald had a real need and that I was not being conned. I supposed it would be alright if my wife logged onto the ALDOC website and sent him a little money every now and then. Technically, I was not giving him money and was not breaking the rules. He was working hard to promote my ministry, so I would help him out and reward him for his service to the Lord.

Just as my ministry was in full swing, somehow the prison found out that I had been giving Donald money and the captain called me in to give me a warning that if I did it again, I would be banned from entering the prison. I told him I would not do it anymore. At that point, Donald was told he could not come to any of my meetings or have anything to do with me during my visits. It was very hard on him because I was the closest thing he had to family.

A few weeks later, after finishing my message, a prisoner I had never met asked me to contact his former employer to let them know he was in prison. He explained that he was not able to contact them prior getting locked up and that they would be concerned about him. It just so happened that I knew the couple he worked for in Tuscaloosa, so I made the contact. They were excited to know what happened and asked how to visit the estranged employee. I was happy to assist this inmate and excitedly called Chaplain Lee to ask for visitation information, but he got very quiet and said he would get back to me. The next time that I came to the prison, I was detained out front and called into a meeting with Chaplain Lee and the Prison Sergeant and was interrogated and chastised for contacting someone on behalf of an inmate. I was told that I could have been contacting the inmate's victim unknowingly which would create a liability for the prison. I explained that I knew the people that the inmate was asking me to contact and could not think of any reason for denying the request plus I did not know I was violating policy. The sergeant did not care what I thought, it was my second violation and I was told that I was no longer welcome as a volunteer at the prison. After two years of faithful service, I was banned as a volunteer.

Chaplain Lee explained to me that he was a paid member of the prison staff and that he was obligated to follow protocol which meant he had to report my violation despite his religious convictions. Shortly after I was banned, Chaplain Lee learned that his job performance was under scrutiny. Unlike me, he had followed protocol to a "T", but it did not seem to matter. He was under investigation after reporting some issues he had with other staff to the head warden. The chaplain would later tell me that the level of corruption of his superiors had gotten to the point that protocol did not necessarily apply to those near the top and that anyone who failed to accommodate as demanded would pay the price. The stress of the prison politics was getting to the Chaplain. Even though he never wore a watch, he had a vision of a watch on his wrist and as he wondered about it, he heard God say that it was time, time for him to resign. Shortly after my expulsion, Chaplain Lee joined me in saying goodbye to the Bibb County Correctional Facility.

Presently Donald Butler continues to spread God's word as a witness of God's freedom and forgiveness behind the prison fence. Chaplain Lee is doing well as pastor of a church in Meridian, MS.

Business Returns in 2012

I know it sounds funny, but getting banned from prison was very painful for me. I felt like I had let God and the prisoners down. I had such a tight relationship with Chaplain Lee and was serving God so mightily that I thought I was untouchable. Due to my own poor decisions and actions, my prison ministry came to an abrupt end in the spring of 2012. I learned a hard lesson regarding the importance of obeying the rules and laws of the land or else it would give the enemy a way to discredit valid ministry.

I had grown so used to volunteering that I forgot that I actually had a full-time job. Like it or not, the veneer business was increasing, and I needed to dedicate my time to righting the ship. Ramping up is always harder than slowing down. By the end of 2012, I had so much going on at work that my former level of prison ministry would have been a burden.

The bank that had been carrying me along for the last few years was bought out by larger bank. The banker who had been drafting one forbearance agreement after another which prevented a foreclosure told me that I had better hope for better numbers soon because the management of the new bank had a reputation for liquidating poorly performing assets. As orders began to return, I threw myself wholeheartedly into saving my company. I was able to re-hire key people lost during the recession and before long we were able to get the engine running on all cylinders.

2013 was definitely the start of a new season in my life financially. I did not need to see our financial statements to know that we were finally doing well again. We had cash flow and were paying our bills. The phone was ringing again with customers I had not heard from in years. Most importantly, we were able to get much needed price increases and return to profitability.

It had been over three years since I had given my life unreservedly to Jesus. During this time, I would often have to fight back doubts that God would bring full restoration as he was using me for ministry but seemed to be ignoring my financial woes. My faith had to be strong enough for Sandy and myself because I had to regularly encourage her to remain strong while encouraging myself. In hindsight it was clear that God was teaching us the true meaning of having faith in Him. We were learning to trust in, rely on and adhere to Him and Him alone. We were skating on such thin financial ice that I could see and hear cracks forming under us as the cold water roared in our wake. My intellect could not fathom a rational means of escape, yet it was abundantly clear that God was with me through marvelous demonstrations of his deliverance and healing power. Thankful for the example of Israelites who were making their way to the "promised land" through the desert, I knew that I must not be moved by my desolate surroundings but rather focus on the One who held me up by his Righteous Right Hand. Survive or not I would trust Him.

It would take a miracle to save my company, but I would see first-hand that the arm of God was not too short. I would come to rest in the understanding that God is good and that He is very good at being God. He is not limited by anything or any situation. Reality is that much of what God tells us to do will not make sense, but we must obey because He is God, and God knows best and is able to do exceeding abundantly above all that we ask or think. There is no substitute for real experience, and after walking through dry places, the 23rd Psalm held new relevance to me.

"The Lord is my shepherd; I shall not want.

He maketh me to lie down in green pastures: he leadeth me beside the still waters.

He restoreth my soul: he leadeth me in the paths of righteousness for his name's sake.

Yea, though I walk through the valley of the shadow of death, I will fear no evil: for thou art with me; thy rod and thy staff they comfort me.

Thou preparest a table before me in the presence of mine enemies: thou anointest my head with oil; my cup runneth over.

Surely goodness and mercy shall follow me all the days of my life: and I will dwell in the house of the Lord for ever."

I now knew that it was not the thickness of the ice that mattered but the hand that I clung to and as long as I held his hand, He would keep my nose above the water.

Perfect Storm

A perfect storm was forming in the veneer business. Veneer supply was down and flooring demand was picking up. There were new flooring manufacturers looking for veneers and there were several of my competitors who did not survive. During the downturn, two large flooring companies opted to close down their in-house veneer factories. These facilities would never again re-open because all the equipment had been liquidated or sold off as scrap. These conditions created excessive demand on the veneer supply. Large flooring companies were concerned that they would not have the veneer they needed to produce their products. Veneer market conditions resulted in a seller's market unlike any I had seen in my lifetime.

Cahaba Veneer had gone international. One of our flooring customers built a flooring plant in China to manufacture labor intensive flooring products with a "hand hewn" look where each plank required intense carving by hand. As a manufacturer who had seen much of his business disappear to China, my attitude toward China had not been positive. Interestingly, my mindset changed dramatically after my conversion. I suddenly had a heart for Chinese missions and looked for a way to use my business to promote ministry there. Visiting customers would be easy enough, but I had no idea how I would get plugged into ministry there. I had never been on any mission trip before and considering the sensitivity of the Chinese government to religious activities I wondered how God would pull it off.

Sandy and I were attending the Tuscaloosa Vineyard church, pastored by Jon Quitt. One Sunday a former missionary to China, Richard Davis, introduced himself. He ended up taking an administrative job in my company and his first task was to plan a two week trip where we would visit some flooring accounts but the rest of the time would be to travel all around China visiting his former ministry contacts and students.

We flew into Beijing, checked into our hotel, and the next day toured the Great Wall, Tianamen Square and The Forbidden City. The day after we flew to Shenyang to visit with one of one of Richard's former students who was part of a ministry there. We had a blast sharing with the class there for several days. Of course I was sharing my heart of freedom through forgiveness, and I was thrilled with the hunger for God in the hearts of the listeners.

Late one evening after returning to our Shenyang Holiday Inn hotel room, I connected to WIFI and got an email that froze me in my tracks. Was this some sort of bad joke? My plant manager said that there had been a catastrophic failure with our boiler. He wrote that he tried to call me but resorted to an email when I did not answer. He said he was not sure of the extent of the damage but that the boiler had been heated without water in the pipes for an extended time and got very hot before cold water was pumped back in. This type of condition could have resulted in a major explosion. Nobody was hurt, but the boiler was inoperable. He would update me as soon as he had more information. I was stunned. I had never had a major boiler failure, but I knew what it meant for my company. We burned wood waste in our boiler to generate steam which was necessary for our processing. Without a boiler the mill would be crippled. I felt totally helpless. I was halfway around the world and still trying to adjust to the time change. I needed answers, and I needed them right away. I counted thirteen hours back and realized that nobody would be awake at home for a few more hours. Immediately my thoughts went to the Lord and I began to speak to Him, "Lord, how could you let this happen to me? After all, I am way over here doing your work." After letting it all sink in, I got my head straight, came to my senses, and confessed that I would trust Him through this situation just as I had through all the rest. I repeated over and over that I did not know how He was going to do it but that I knew He was going to do it. God said it and that was enough even though I could not imagine any of this turning out to be good. "The steps of a good man are ordered by the Lord: and he delighteth in his way." Psalm 37:23. This was another big problem, but I had the same, much bigger God. "And we know that all things work together for good to them that love God, to them who are the called according to his purpose." Romans 8:28.

To begin with, I was hoping for an easy fix. I thought that maybe my staff had over-reacted and that it was not as bad as it sounded and it could be fixed in a reasonable amount of time and get the plant back up to speed. I did my best to think positively about the situation, but it was not easy with such a large knot in my stomach. When I shared the news with Richard, he excitedly offered to book a flight for me on the next plane home. He was only trying to be helpful, but he began to irritate me with his repeated offers to expedite my return home. He was working for me, and I was paying for the trip, yet he was asking to put me on the next plane home while he finished out the remainder of our itinerary. I was fighting the urge to react out of fear, and I needed to keep a cool head to properly process how to best respond, so I told him that I would let him know if I wanted to change my plans.

A few hours later, the sun rose on the West and I got an update from my plant manager. The news was not good. Many of the boiler tubes which were supposed to hold water were ruptured, and there would be no easy fix. Before leaving for China, I had three weeks of production and shipping schedules all planned out. All of that was out the window. I now had to report to customers and develop a new strategy for continued production. Sandy was shell-shocked. She was being asked a lot of questions the answers for which she did not have, and I think she was starting to miss me. I was able to work out a revised production schedule on my laptop and send it back home that would allow the veneer mill to limp along without the use of our boiler.

The million dollar question was whether or not the damages to my boiler would be covered by insurance. This question called for a lot of prayer. A few days later I was told that it was covered and the adjuster recommended that I rent a boiler to fully restore operations. I also had business income loss insurance which covers lost income due during times like these so it was important to my insurance carrier that operations be fully restored as soon as possible to minimize the claim. After some late night discussions with Mark Hutter of ADCO Boiler Company in Birmingham it was determined that ADCO could supply a natural gas fired boiler that was large enough to get us all the steam we needed. ADCO also represented the brand of boiler that we had just wrecked and they were working to provide permanent options for replacement or repair. All things considered, I believed that there was not much more that I could have done even if I was in Alabama. With any luck, the temporary boiler would be hooked up and have the mill running at normal capacity by the time I got home.

The balance of my time in China was very rewarding. We had two good customer visits, but most of our time was spent sharing our hearts for the Lord. The highlight of my trip was our time spent in Shanghai. The wood flooring factories to which we sold veneer were located on the outskirts of Shanghai. Shanghai no doubt has the largest population of any city I have ever visited, which tops 23 million. For a small town boy like me, this was quite a sight. It seemed like the city never ended. Richard and I had very little down time when we were not speaking or visiting customers but we had nothing lined up for our last few days in Shanghai so we thought we would be able to do some touristy stuff. Richard had no known ministry connections in Shanghai. At the last minute, one of his former students, Peter, sent him a message that he was working in Shanghai for a large Christian ministry and would like to see us. Shortly thereafter Peter came to our hotel for a meet and greet. Before he left, I gave him a copy of *When Pigs Move In* by Don Dickerman as a gift for his ministry leader. Later that morning we were invited to speak to a group of eager Bible school students in a high rise condominium somewhere in the heart of Shanghai. Richard spoke first for a few hours and I went second. The students wanted prayer afterwards and we prayed for them individually. As we prayed for these young men and women, they began to faint backwards and had to be caught before they hit the floor. I had seen it before but had always wondered if it was legitimate.

It would be several years later before I knew the truth about how we were able to gain the trust of the underground church in Shanghai and readily welcomed as guest speakers. The senior Chinese pastor, Dr. Joshua Yang, thought I was Don Dickerman.

On the 24 hour trip home, my mind was often on the boiler situation that was waiting for me. I remembered a phone conversation I had a week or two before leaving for China that made me scratch my head. It was with Bobby Bright, a veneer and plywood expert of sorts from Molino, Florida who had helped me oversee several mill projects. He had not worked for me in years, and we were just catching up. Out of the blue he brought up that I was going to need to do something about my boiler because it was old, and in his opinion would give me trouble before too long. I responded that I did not have a million dollars to replace it with and that it would have to do for now.

When I got back home, the temporary gas boiler was on-site and being connected. A few days later we turned it on but quickly discovered that our gas supply was inadequate to produce the 33 million BTU's the boiler was rated for. The Alabama Gas Company would have to run a larger pipe down our street to get us running normally again but we would soon get there.

The type of wood fired boiler that we wrecked was not very common but it just so happened that ADCO had a Nebraska boiler vessel in stock in Birmingham that was a very close match to my wrecked Cleaver-Brooks model. After all was said and done, by September I had a refurbished boiler and the total insurance claim was about a million dollars. I will never forget the depth of despair that I felt when I got the news of the boiler disaster in Shenyang. Thankfully, I had a foundation of faith in God and He continued to prove Himself trustworthy. Not only did I get a new boiler, but I am still reaping the tax savings today from the depreciation expense of the cost of the boiler replacement even though most of it was paid by insurance. I have come to delight in the following verses: Psalm 34:19, "Many are the afflictions of the righteous: but the LORD delivereth him out of them all." and Genesis 50:20, "But as for you, ye thought evil against me; but God meant it unto good, to bring to pass, as it is this day, to save much people alive."

Restorations

In 2013, Business was going so well that my bank restored my account to normal status and offered to refinance my debt at a lower rate. By September I was able to negotiate two contracts with two flooring customers that would result in guaranteed record sales that far exceeded all pre-recession levels.

My relationship with Sandy has flourished. God is no doubt continuing to work on me, and I have been amazed as I watch God transform Sandy more closely to His image right before my eyes. We have not been without challenges, but I am convinced that every marriage requires a tremendous reliance on God to get it through difficult situations. The fact that we rely on Him to meet all our needs has made all the difference as we get ready to celebrate our 6th anniversary in a few weeks.

Dealing with children of your own is tough, but stepchildren with attitudes are a whole different degree of difficulty. That being said, giving them to the Lord resulted in the same positive outcome as all the other challenges that we have faced. Sandy and her girls are very close and Sandy's main struggle today is separation anxiety. Her oldest daughter plans to leave Tuscaloosa this fall to continue her studies in Psychology at a grad school in North Carolina. Only God could have repaired the stumbling blocks that once stood between me and Sandy's children. We get along very well, and they know that I sincerely love them.

As far as the twins, they are now 18 and about to graduate from high school. They are tall and slim like their father and are absolutely gorgeous. I am very proud of them. Their behavior is exemplary and they have done well in school. When they became seniors, I decided to release them from the obligation to see me every other weekend. They have busier schedules than I could imagine so I just let them come when they want. It has been very rewarding to see them continue to take time for me and value our relationships. I did everything I could to prove to them that I loved them through many years of struggling with their mother for parental rights. It has been quite some time since there was apparent tension between Sandy and the twins on their visits, and the girls have always gotten along well among their stepsisters.

Audra remains a challenge but I see signs of breakthrough there too. She has dated several men through the years yet remains unmarried. The twins said that she did not want to introduce another man to their household until they graduated and went off to college. I respect her for that. She appears to be serious with her boyfriend, and it is my prayer that she will move forward in a healthy marital relationship. My hope is that she will come to a place of forgiveness and peace that comes only from her maker.

No matter what challenge I have faced or will face, I don't know how He is going to do it, but I know He is going to do it as long as I continue to walk in love as commanded.

Generational Sin: My Father's Schizophrenia

From what I can tell, the illness hit my father at about the time that he and my mother got married catching him by surprise. He chose to save face by doing the best he could to hide it from my mother. He dragged her all over the southern U.S., but maybe there was a method to his madness after all. I believe that he recognized the voices in his head as evil spirits and was seeking help along those lines when he enrolled into Presbyterian seminary in Austin, Texas. Many years later, my mother learned that he was kicked out of the seminary after failing a psychological evaluation—one that his parents knew of but chose not to share with her. All he told my mom was that it was not working for him. After his illness prevented him from doing a proper job as a history professor in Georgia, he then sought his masters in psychology. I suspect that he might have been trying to hold his marriage and family together while figuring out what was going on in his head with that degree as well. He had run out of options before being forced into the private sector with the announcement of my sister.

I am fairly certain that the mental illness that came upon my father when he was about twenty years old was the result of generational sin. You can be sure that I have looked as far into my family history as I could to see if anyone stood out as a possible cause. According to the Bible, to review all the possible people who could have contributed to passing a curse down to us, we have to look back four generations to our great-great grandparents. We have 16 great-great grandparents and 8 great grandparents. If you are like me, you know very little about any of them. There are only a few of that group of twenty four that I would feel remotely comfortable in guessing if they lived a life of servitude to God or rebellious life of sin.

There are two main problems with conducting such an investigation. First of all, such information does not normally get passed down because most people prefer to keep skeletons of their heritage locked in a closet. Secondly, our great and great-great grandparents make up over 80% of the group. For most of us, this group of 24 of the possible 30 people have long since been dead and they are the most difficult to acquire information on. Our grandparents may resist the request for such information on their parents or grandparents. If your grandparents are still living, that may be your only chance to learn key information about your heritage.

In my search, I have a hunch of what might have caused the curse to come down. Both great-grandfathers on the Givhan side were involved in freemasonry which was very popular during their time, but it appears that my grandmother's father, John Ramsey Lewis, was especially into it. It is unfair to call him out because I really do not know where the curse came from. He is just my first guess. Considering the historical prominence of other groups, such as the KKK among southerners, it would not surprise me if some of my ancestors were involved in that hateful group. I suppose that being a zealous leader or member of this group would draw special ire from God. It is not wise to falsely represent His symbol of unconditional love by burning it in a display of racial hatred for those He loves and considers His children.

The good news is that knowledge of my ancestry is nothing more than interesting information. It does not matter who they were or what they did. The only thing we need to know is that Jesus died on the cross and was cursed for us so that the curse that has come down to us can be removed by believing and claiming it in Jesus' name.

Parting Thoughts

When the head pastor of our church promoted my freedom ministry from the pulpit, it was not long before one of the junior pastors, Jonathan Cook, asked if we could meet for coffee. I had not been formally introduced to him but I had heard him speak several times. I thought him to be intelligent and looked forward to getting to know him even though he seemed to be a little standoffish. As we sat down with our coffee outside Starbucks, he got right to business with a question that told me everything I needed to know about his motive for the meeting. He asked me if I was one of those people who thought demons were hiding under every rock. After checking his face for signs of humor and finding none, I responded that no I was not because as far as I knew none of them needed to hide under a rock. He then laughed and said, "Yeah well I was just wondering if you were one of those people who would try to blame every problem on a demon." At that point we both laughed as I said that we humans were well capable of creating plenty of problems of our own without assistance from demons.

While there is no doubt many superstitious people who would like to blame all their mistakes and problems on dark supernatural powers beyond their control, the biblical reality is that we are individually responsible for our actions, regardless of how much evil coercion we receive. Demons don't care what excuse we give as long as we continue in our sin. Demons are formidable under-cover agents who wield tremendous experience and mental agility. Close attention must be paid to God's Word or our ignorance makes us easy prey to these resourceful schemers. Once we are in bondage, as the term suggests, we truly can say that the devil made us do it. However, even as slaves to sin, we are nonetheless responsible because the devil was able to get control only because we or our ancestors opened the door, invited them in and gave it to them. Once they get control, they will work relentlessly to maintain it.

I would prefer that people looked for the devils in their details, even if wrongly motivated. At least these types believe that a spiritual element is at play. It is an even greater danger for us to put our heads in the sand while wrestling with powers of darkness. Ephesians 6 does not portray our enemies as creatures who hide under rocks but as well-organized, highly supervised and strategically placed creatures that engage with us in very close combat.

When I was in the 7th grade, I was on the Warrior Academy wrestling team. This was collegiate style wrestling and not the staged professional variety. I was a very active child and loved to compete in all sorts of sports. Coach Tidmore was an imposing hulk of man who worked us out like our lives depended on the outcome of our next match. The physical conditioning was simply grueling. When we were not learning wrestling moves or practicing against one another, we ran lap after lap around the gym. As we ran, he would take turns pulling us to the side to watch us climb a fat rope that was suspended from the gym ceiling. Such preparation was not without reason because competition involved concentrated levels of continuous exertion. Once opponents were writhing and struggling on the mat, being in proper shape was necessary or exhaustion would come in a matter of seconds.

A good wrestler is part defense and part opportunist. Competitors seek desperately to keep from being overcome while searching for weaknesses or waiting for a mistake from their opponent. There would be no sense in attempting a move until the opposition showed a weakness and when they did, it was time to attack.

As a 7th grader I was a tall and very skinny 100 pounder. Regardless of how much I worked out or how many protein shakes I drank, my genetics dictated I would never be bulky but I was stubbornly competitive, agile and wiry. When we competed against other schools, I was in the 105 pound weight class which meant that neither my competitor nor I could weigh over 105 pounds, regardless of age. Weight rules were strict and every wrestler would have to be weighed in just before the match. At the end of the season, our team went to the state meet which would settle who were the state champions across Alabama private schools for the various weight classes. I went undefeated until the final match which would determine who would be the 105 pound champion. Unlike most of the other competition I faced, this guy was different. He weighed less than 105 pounds but he was much older than me. He was a petite 18 year old senior. The advantage he held over me was obvious. While I gave him a good match, it was his knowledge and experience that gave him advantage. For the first time all season, I found my back firmly pinned to the mat with an unsatisfactory second place medal.

No other sport involves the level of intimacy that wrestling does. Germaphobes would not dare take up this sport. Well matched competitors are guaranteed the exchange of sweat and spit with the possibility of blood. To achieve victory by pinning your competitor means putting him flat on his back as you hold him there chest to chest. An ancient sport, wrestling is believed to be the oldest of all sports with archaeological evidence dating it back over 4,000 years. With a few restrictions, opponents have free range to manipulate one another any way they can to gain advantage and ultimately submission. Wrestling is how God describes our struggle against our spiritual enemies. Our opponents have been at it for a very long time. The stakes in this sport are real and our lives depend on how well we compete. To overcome we must first acknowledge that we are grappling with enemies who desire to control us and ultimately pin us firmly in Hell. Demons are always close by and are carefully examining every possible weakness for exploitation. Second, if we are to avoid being taken down by these stealthy enemies, we must allow God to give us proper training and get us in shape to compete. Our coach and example is the best there ever was or ever will be and His name is Jesus. He is undefeated and his record is flawless. He knows all the moves and weaknesses of our enemies. He pinned the devil and now desires to share his Holy Spirit with us so that we might have the same power within us that enabled Him to rise victoriously. We must listen to our Coach and do what he says.

Bondage comes only when permission is granted by God. Demons know very well what conditions must be met in order to gain permission and are strategically placed around us, constantly hoping for a condition to be met that would allow them the pleasure of occupancy and control. Most of the time they get permission on account of our sin.

The very first example of this in the Bible is found in Genesis 4:7, where God explains the situation to Cain. Cain's sacrifice to God was not accepted and he was offended that Abel's was. As Cain contemplated what to do with this offense, God tried to intervene before Cain sinned. Of course Cain did not heed God's warning which resulted in the murder of Abel and a horrible curse upon Cain's life.

> "If thou doest well, shalt thou not be accepted? And if thou doest not well, sin lieth at the door. And unto thee Shall be his desire and thou shalt rule over him." (Genesis 4:7)

Generational Sin: We are all born with sin that has come to us from our ancestors. The Bible teaches that generational sin is sin that we become responsible for—even though we did not do it. Part of our ancestors' punishment is that we are cursed at birth with sin or demonic bondage on account of the evil they did. It may seem unfair, but it is a spiritual law that God punishes the children of those who hate him by passing their sin (demonic bondage) down to the third and fourth generation. This is known as the generational curse. Going back four generations, chances are very good that some of our thirty ancestors who contributed to our DNA have passed down various tendencies that are ungodly. We see an example of this being displayed in John 9 when the disciples asked Jesus if a man was blind on account of his sin or his parent's sin. From this exchange it was clear that Jesus had been teaching his disciples about the generational curse. Bottom line, we inherit sin and demonic bondage from our ancestors.

The wide road is full of people who think their sinful tendencies just run in the family and accept them because they believe God made them that way. While it is true that we are born in demonic bondage to sin, it would be a fatal mistake to assume that it was God's intent for us to remain that way or that He will overlook it on Judgement Day. The Bible does not support that understanding. The truth is that Jesus died that we might be forgiven and have spiritual rebirth. 1 John 5:18 clearly says, "We know that whosoever is born of God sinneth not; but that he is begotten of God keepeth himself, and that wicked one toucheth him not." Jesus clearly states that the person He sets free is really free. I am not saying that any of us will get to a place of absolute perfection, but I am saying that the mistakes we made yesterday cannot be repeated over and over again. Future sins must be unintentional, honest mistakes and not the ones we were warned of an hour ago. Sanctification is a process for sure, but as we spin on the potter's wheel, our appearance must become more and more like the image of Christ or else our potter is most likely a wolf in shepherd's clothing. God is patient to give us ample time to resolve our differences, but all sin must be treated with extreme prejudice. Jesus repeated himself twice in Matthew chapters 5 and 18 with stern warnings about sin. He said that if your eye causes you to sin, pluck it out or if you hand or foot causes you to sin then cut it off because it would be better to enter life blind or cripple than enter hell with all your members. We must not allow sinful lifestyles, secretly promoted by demons, to continue their carnage in us and the lives of our children because eternity is at stake.

Your deliverance means freedoms for your children too. Most parents strive their entire lives to give their children a better life than they have had. We want to see all their talents discovered and developed to maximum potential. We want our children to live life to the fullest. Yet, unless we allow Jesus to clean out our spiritual houses, our Children will inherit a bunch of spiritual junk from us that they will have a hard time getting rid of. Jesus says it best.

> "The thief cometh not, but for to steal, and to kill, and to destroy: I am come that they might have life, and that they might have it more abundantly." John 10:10

This statement indicates that the life we want for ourselves and our children comes only through Jesus and his protection from evil. Parents must, of course, make it a top priority to care for the various needs of their children but what if people understood that the best gift that could be given to their children was a healthy spiritual inheritance. Many parents may understand this principle but are unaware of how to make it happen. It happens when the parents find freedom which results in freedom and blessings on the children of those who love God to a thousand generations. What an awesome opportunity parents have to be a blessing to their children that far exceeds in value any temporary worldly gifts. We must put God first and let Him be concerned with the adding of all other things. When we are focused on giving our children more and more stuff, all we do is spoil them and our good intentions end with poor results. On the other hand, passing down the generational blessing greatly enhances their ability to make their own way with God's favor on their lives. It leads to wise decisions which affects every area of their lives and of course the greatest benefit of all, eternal life. When we get free, our freedom results in freedom for our children and the benefits flow down to a thousand generations of those who love God.

New sins: Other than what we have inherited, we have ample opportunity to embrace new sin which leads to new bondages of our own which further complicate our already complex generational heritage. Generational demons we are born with are tasked with further promoting other sin with new demonic entrants to further entangle their victim. Simply put, one sin leads to another. One demon leads to another. The good news is that Jesus came to deal with it all. He came to give us a new heart and new born again spirit and spiritual health to pass down to our children. In the following passage the apostle Paul discusses the before and after deliverance.

"For we know that the law is spiritual: but I am carnal, sold under sin. For that which I do I allow not: for what I would, that do I not; but what I hate, that do I. If then I do that which I would not, I consent unto the law that it is good. Now then it is no more I that do it, but sin that dwelleth in me. For I know that in me (that is, in my flesh,) dwelleth no good thing: for to will is present with me; but how to perform that which is good I find not. For the good that I would I do not: but the evil which I would not, that I do. Now if I do that I would not, it is no more I that do it, but sin that dwelleth in me… O wretched man that I am! who shall deliver me from the body of this death? I thank God through Jesus Christ our Lord. So then with the mind I myself serve the law of God; but with the flesh the law of sin." Romans 7:14-20, 24, 25

Jesus desires to deliver us from the evil that so easily entangles and set us free indeed!

The Fruit of Forgiveness

In my mother's initial prophetic Word from God, God tells me, "Forgiveness is a fruit I want to give you. This fruit makes everything sweet in your life. When you give it away—it sets you free." When I first read that, I had no clue what it meant. At this point, I understand God's will for my life involves educating people in the importance of walking in unconditional love and forgiveness. Simply put, my passion is to help others forgive because when they give it away, it sets them free. In the gospels, Jesus teaches that his disciples must bear good fruit. I believe that true believers will all bear good fruit of various types. The fruit that I am called to bear is that of forgiveness, and I hope that by my testimony you have been inspired to give forgiveness a new place of importance in your life—because your eternal life depends on it.

Most people seem to be endowed with a basic sense of right and wrong regardless of cultural background. To rely solely upon instinctual perceptions of morality is to err greatly. What seems right often does not accurately follow the rule of law.

> Proverbs 14:12 and 16:25, "There is a way which seemeth right unto a man, but the end thereof are the ways of death."

The Righteous Judge sent his son that He might clarify misunderstandings of God's law and empower us to follow Him in proper obedience. The primary theme of the gospel of Jesus Christ is forgiveness and unconditional love. One may come to proper understanding of unforgiveness as sin only through the revelation of God and His word. Common moral understandings reflect obligations of retribution rather than forgiveness of offenses. Consequently unforgiveness is a trap that many have fallen victim to. Ignorance of this flaw in the conscience of man results in a devastating doorway of demonic entry resulting in untold damage.

We need forgiveness, and therefore we must forgive all others, including ourselves. No Bible believing Christian should be surprised that our spiritual enemies are scheming for ways to draw us into sin. Jesus taught us that unforgiveness is a major type of sin and wickedness. This is revealed in Matthew 18:32-35.

> [32] Then his lord, after that he had called him, said unto him, O thou wicked servant, I forgave thee all that debt, because thou desiredst me:
>
> [33] Shouldest not thou also have had compassion on thy fellowservant, even as I had pity on thee?
>
> [34] And his lord was wroth, and delivered him to the tormentors, till he should pay all that was due unto him.
>
> [35] So likewise shall my heavenly Father do also unto you, if ye from your hearts forgive not every one his brother their trespasses.

Considering that the sin of unforgiveness is guaranteed by God's Word to bring demonic torment (ver. 35) and interrupts our forgiveness from God (Matt 6:14-15), we can rest assured that our spiritual enemies are continually striving to catch us in snares of unforgiveness and offense. Forgiveness is not reconciliation with the offender, nor is it to say that the offense is acceptable. It is to come into obedience with your maker, who reserves rights to vengeance as His own. Resolve to adopt a spirit of Love such that nobody owes you anything and that you are only God's servant. Pray this simple prayer to get freedom now.

> "Lord, your word says that you will not forgive me unless I first forgive everyone who has ever offended me. I choose to forgive all others including myself. Please show me if there is anyone that you would like for me to specifically forgive…(pause and give the Holy Spirit a moment to give you specific names). I am only your servant and I release him/her to you (repeat this for each person he gives you, sincerely from the heart). Lord, I now ask you to forgive me of my trespasses and deliver me from evil. I bind all spirits of evil that have attached themselves to me and I cancel your rights to me and my family in Jesus' name. Any of yourselves that you have passed down to my children, I command that you call back and take them with you right now in Jesus Name. After you have restored all the damage that you have done in me and my children, go directly into the pit, never again to return right now in Jesus name. "

My prayer is that my testimony has inspired you and will result in supernatural protections for you and your family for many generations.

"And the son said unto him, Father, I have sinned against heaven, and in thy sight, and am no more worthy to be called thy son. But the father said to his servants, Bring forth the best robe, and put it on him; and put a ring on his hand, and shoes on his feet: And bring hither the fatted calf, and kill it; and let us eat, and be merry: For this my son was dead, and is alive again; he was lost, and is found. And they began to be merry." (Luke 15:21-24)

* * *

My mother's note from the Lord says that books, plural, would be written. Yes, I plan to write more. It was my intent to introduce myself and my ministry in this, my first book. Going forward, I plan to provide detailed Bible analysis and explanations along with corresponding real world stories of people finding freedom. It was also my intent to cause you to ask questions and search the scriptures on your own. My next book will hopefully address some of these questions.

If you have topics that you would like for me to discuss in future publications, you may go to www.theprodigaldeliverer.com and click the "Tell Me More" link to submit the topic(s) that you would like for me to discuss further.

To receive updates regarding future publications, sign up for my newsletter on the website and I will let you know when my next book is available.

If this book has been a blessing to you, please go to www.amazon.com and leave a review so that others might influenced to read this book and get free!

God Bless!

Pete

Made in the USA
San Bernardino, CA
16 July 2017